MAKING
CHANGE WORK

For a complete list of Management Books 2000 titles,
visit our web-site at http://www.mb2000.com

MAKING CHANGE WORK

Edgar Wille
Philip Hodgson
and
you

2000

First edition published 1991

Second edition published 2000 by Management Books 2000 Ltd
Reprinted 2005 by Management Books 2000 Ltd
Forge House, Limes Road
Kemble, Cirencester
Gloucestershire, GL7 6AD
Tel. 01285-771441 Fax: 01285-771055
e-mail: info@mb2000.com
Website: www.mb2000.com

Printed and bound in Great Britain by Digital Books Logistics of Peterborough

British Library Cataloguing in Publication Data is available

ISBN 1-85252-365-4

CONTENTS

HOW TO USE THIS BOOK

You as co-author

You will have noticed that the title page of this book includes you, the reader, as one of the co-authors. This is partly true of all books, at least those which sound the call to thought and action – the reader engages in discussion with the author(s), debate goes on within the reader's mind – and this book is a call to thought and action.

But in its very structure this book invites you to join in the writing of it. Every now and again we leave a blank section for you to contribute your own experience to the matter in hand. We see a book as a tool to be used in learning, and improved by the marginal notes of the reader. (We try to resist this temptation when borrowing a book, though we are reminded of Charles Lamb's comment that when you lent a book to Samuel Taylor Coleridge, it always came back immeasurably enriched by marginal comments; but even Coleridge might have got into trouble if he had done this to a library book.) If you feel it is a sacrilege to write in a book or if you are a borrower, then we suggest you take an exercise book, head it up 'Making Change Work', and turn it into Volume 2 of this book.

Whichever way you choose, we do hope you will join us in the authorship and record your experiences of:

- Personal change – Chapter 2
- Global changes in your lifetime – Chapter 3
- Business changes you have experienced – Chapter 6
- Business changes you would like to see – Chapter 8

[1]

- Power you had and exercised – Chapter 9
- Little things that made a difference – Chapter 10
- Traumatic change from which you recovered – Chapter 11

Structure of this book

The impetus for this book came from the programme 'Making Change Work' in which we are both involved at Ashridge. As this is a book, the structure is different, but much of the core thinking is the same. We have not divided this book into parts, because we want it to be seen as a unity, yet it does fall naturally into the three closely linked sections set out below, which are followed by the key thought of each chapter:

Chapters 1–6 CHANGE: principles and context	Chapters 7–8 CHANGE: stories and examples	Chapters 9–14 CHANGE: skills and approaches
1 Change as a way of life	7 Examples of change from the Ashridge Change Data Base	9 You have power to change things
2 Personal experience of change		10 Little things make a difference
3 Global background of change	8 Recent visits to companies in change	11 Change can hurt but you'll survive
4 Living in the future now		12 Overcoming resistance to change
5 Key change themes		13 Skills you need in change situations
6 How business changes		14 Successful organisations learn all the time

Purpose of this book

We hope that you will:

- enjoy it
- enter into debate and co-authorship with us
- be able to welcome and control change
- find opportunities for beneficial change everywhere
- understand the world and your environment a little better
- be inspired by stories of successful change
- realise your own power to change things
- recognise the value of small changes
- learn better to survive unwelcome change
- go out and practise new skills
- help your organisation by continuous feedback and improvement to become a learning organisation
- expand your earning power and your enjoyment of work

Welcome

So we welcome you to the co-operative task of relating with the parts of this book that are written and yourself writing the parts that aren't. Whatever your level of operation in your enterprise, we hope you will be encouraged to seize opportunities even from unexpected sources and to share with us the sense of adventure implicit in all change. We hope you will, in the words of our title, 'make change work'.

Edgar Wille
Phil Hodgson

ACKNOWLEDGEMENTS

We are grateful to so many people for help in one way or another in producing this book: Philip Sadler, former Chief Executive of Ashridge, for suggesting the book; Peter Needham of Ashridge Management College for practical support; Gill Russell, Barbara Gregory, Liz Stedman of Ashridge, Karen Yule and Karen Watts for the word processing; Kevin Barham and Valerie Hammond of Ashridge Management Research Group for the use of the Ashridge Change Data Base and help in current research on management development; and Peter Beddowes of Ashridge Consultancy Group for sponsoring 'Triggers for Change', on which Chapter 7 is based, and Robin Ladkin and Bill Critchley for many hours of fruitful debate around the 'Making Change Work' programme we run at Ashridge.

We thank the management of companies referred to in Chapter 8 for opening the doors, members of the Management Charter Initiative Network for giving us contacts, Bill Pryce of the Training Agency for help in the search for the relationship between management development and improved business performance.

We know we've missed people out, because sometimes it's just a chance remark that changes a whole perception, and though you reap the harvest, you can't remember the sower. So we thank all who have changed us at any stage of our lives, and, in advance, those who will continue to change us.

Finally, we both want to recognise and thank our families for the support they have given us during the months of writing this book and the decades of preparation for it.

Edgar Wille
Phil Hodgson

[4]

Chapter 1

DEVELOPING THE CHANGE MINDSET

'The times they are a changing', sang Bob Dylan, and 'more's the pity' perhaps you say. Perhaps you are a manager in a manufacturing or service company or a public authority, and 'they' won't let you alone to get on with things. Always something new is coming in, the organisation is restructured, the company gets taken over, or new government regulations or deregulation come in and change everything. Change – it's the one aspect of life that never seems to change. It happens all the time. The only thing is that there seems to be more of it and it happens more and more quickly. There's never time to catch your breath.

You are then totally fed up with change. 'There is no stability nowadays.' 'You no sooner get things sorted out and there is a restructuring, a product change or a new competitor running away with our business.' 'You just get the line running smoothly and rejects to a minimum when in comes some new technology or a new product is introduced and chaos is let loose.' You sigh for the old days when you knew where you were; yes, things did change then, but much more steadily. You had time to absorb the changes – or so you think now.

This book aims to help you or all the different yous who may read it to come to terms with change. Further than that, we have the outrageous aim to help you actually to welcome change and improve your own prospects and that of your enterprise by seeking change, creating change and even loving change.

What is management?

You are a manager. What does this mean? The word derives from the ancient French word for handling horses and a later one for handling the affairs of the kitchen. Cynics might replace horse by donkey, but all would see the analogy of keeping an organisation alive through the activities of the kitchen.

What is management? Edgar has a favourite definition which emerged from a learning session he led:

'Management is risking yourself in the mobilisation of resources and relationships to add value to the enterprise.'

Every phrase was debated and agonised over for a long period.

Risking yourself
Every time you make a decision you risk yourself. You chop off one branch of a tree in favour of another. That is the meaning of the word 'decide', from the Latin *decidere*, meaning to cut off. It's a risky business, because you can't easily stick back the branch you have chopped off.

Mobilising resources
Nothing happens without resources; there are never enough of them and they won't always readily provide the advantage that you seek. So there are people, materials, money, markets, ideas, components, space and time and many other resources all requiring to be mobilised before you can produce and sell what you have to offer. The word 'mobilise' has a very active ring about it, and management is about activity.

Mobilising relationships
Edgar used the definition without this phrase at first. Then David Cox, who used to be managing director of Ind Coope Brewery in Burton and successfully established team working there, pointed out that mobilising resources would only take you so far unless you got the relationships right, especially those of people. People meant workforce, suppliers, customers, shareholders, government, community – all the stakeholders. They had to be given a sense of sharing ownership for what was

[6]

going on – and managers were the prime influences of this process. They were people-linkers.

To add value

We could have said profit, and often this is what we mean. But we can be in the voluntary or the public sector where the community has to be served, effectively and economically, but where it has been decided by the government or people or both that the activity must be run outside the normal market mechanisms of shareholders and stock markets. We are dodging the debate, feeling that to add value covers all kinds of business activity.

To the enterprise

Not 'organisation' or 'firm' or 'business' or 'company'. All these would be perfectly appropriate, but we wanted a word that would have a forceful, thrusting, innovative, creative, exciting flavour, and enterprise seems to capture that approach.

Your power as a manager

So, as a manager, you are almost bound to participate in the processes of change in the enterprise for which you work. But how? In your company you may feel that you have little chance to influence the process of change. All the decisions are taken at the very top and what the chief executive says is final. So the change decisions are handed down and you have to get on with handling and implementing them.

But surely you will still have an effect on how the company or enterprise performs in the implementing of change? Everyone in any enterprise is involved in change in some way or other, and its success or failure depends on everyone. The ideal company may well consult a large number of its employees about decisions concerning change – what to change, how to change and when to change. If it does, its employees will have a sense of ownership in the changes and are more likely to co-operate in their implementation. Of course there are, in even the most participative of companies, situations where there is no time to consult everybody or where secrecy is of the essence, such as in

[7]

some merger or acquisition decisions. And some companies are just autocratic anyway.

But whatever the situation, at all levels every manager has some contribution to make to the process of change; and to make that contribution requires a certain attitude of mind – a certain mindset. To identify this mindset, and to assist its growth in the readers and indeed in the enterprise for which they work, is the purpose of this book. Since there is so much written about change that is defensive, we thought it was time to present a positive angle to help managers at all levels to welcome change, to embrace it, to be looking out for it all the time, to be recognising it as the very heart of life in general and business life in particular.

Change at the heart of life

We really mean that change is at the very heart of life. Think about it for a moment, independent of business as such, and look at the role of change in general. You could say that life *is* change. From conception to death we are changing physically every microsecond, and certainly from the first moment of independent existence we are changing mentally, emotionally and spiritually. Physically we know that in every seven year period every molecule of our body has changed, very slowly and gradually, and we are certainly not the persons we were. Similarly we are not the same in our mental, emotional and spiritual senses.

For one thing, in every waking moment, and probably when we are asleep as well, we are taking in new impressions and rearranging the old impressions in the light of the new, so that there is no such thing as stability. Neither would we want there to be. Several significant schools of philosophic thought have stressed this.

Life as process

The celebrated mathematician and philosopher Alfred North Whitehead spent most of the autumn of his life thinking through what it was to be a human being. His reflections led to the conclusion that a more apt description would be 'human becomings', because we are never in a static state of being but on the move all the time, in process, or changing, every micro-microsecond. His view became known as 'process philosophy'. In his view we are each of us an ongoing series of events, each event springing out of the previous one and all held together by the thread of memory. We have already mentioned the seven year physical change, but it is equally true of the mental that nothing stays still for as much as a second.

We are all the time taking into our minds new impressions through the senses. We see things, we hear things, we smell things, we touch things, we taste things, and beyond that we have feelings about the messages our five senses bring to us. They make us sad, happy, impatient, excited, worried, angry, uplifted, determined, uncertain, jealous, envious; they make us love, hate, sympathise, empathise, co-operate, oppose, fight; and these emotions, being stirred, provide us with energy and impel us to action.

All these impressions and the emotions they stir are recorded in our memories. Everything we have ever seen, heard, tasted, touched, smelt, and the related emotions, are indelibly written down in our human audio–video–taste–tactile–olfactory tape machines, in our brains or at least in our minds, if these are not the same. These data are all getting added to all the time. As more ingredients come in to the mind, so the earlier ones seem just a little different – they are expanded or perceived in a new light.

Of course, if we had the whole of the tape machine playing at once, we should 'go out of our minds', and so memory is selective. The whole range of material is not making its presence felt consciously all the time. A lot of it is buried, as we sometimes say, 'in the depths of the unconscious', but it is still there and gets called up by new events, and by being linked with them it is changed.

Edgar has a vivid experience he quotes to illustrate this:

I had often driven through south-western English country-side along a motorway, usually at high speed with little opportunity to take in the detail. One day I suddenly saw a house that wasn't there any more! I had often passed it and never seen it, or at least not consciously, but now it had been pulled down and I was conscious for the first time of what it had been.

We have an exciting picture of the human mind as a flow of impressions, and emotions and ideas which connect them. The thinking we do about the impressions is part of the change process, because the bringing of things into new connections presents them in new light – indeed changes them.

So if change is the microsecond by microsecond essence of living, our theme of the need for a change mindset should not be difficult to absorb, because it fits with the very structure of our minds and of our thinking.

Life as interaction

A second contributor to this perception of existence is George Henry Mead, late of Chicago University. He lectured much and wrote little, but his students felt that what he was saying was so powerful that they took detailed notes and produced his material so that we, after his death, can reflect upon it. He gave rise to a sociological and psychological theory, academically known as 'symbolic interactionism'.

A major aspect of it is that people interact by symbols – words and non-verbal signals in particular. Every interaction makes a contribution to the mental make-up of the other. When you have had an interaction with someone, you go away a different person. You have each added something to the other. Mead described each individual as having or being a central 'I' around which a whole lot of 'me s' – less stable and derived from the interactions with others – were revolving. The 'I' then constantly reacted to all these constantly changing 'me s' and absorbed them into itself. It was, of course, a concept rather than a literal fact, but when we think about the people who have influenced us and changed us, we know it to be true. You who have read these words, as a result of our interaction, are a slightly different person from the one you were a few moments ago.

So being human and change go together and this should make the quest of this book the easier.

Living experience

There is a third guru who has something to offer on this theme of human becomings and what they become. Fortunately he is very much still with us at the Case Western Reserve University in Cleveland, Ohio. I refer to David Kolb. In mentioning him I come very much closer to our business theme, as that is the area of his academic activity.

He is the formulator of the well-known Kolb Learning Cycle. To sum it up, he says that learning is all about having experiences (in line with Whitehead and Mead, with life as a series of experiences which make us what we are). He goes on to say that the next stage of the cycle or circle or spiral (see Figure 1.1) is

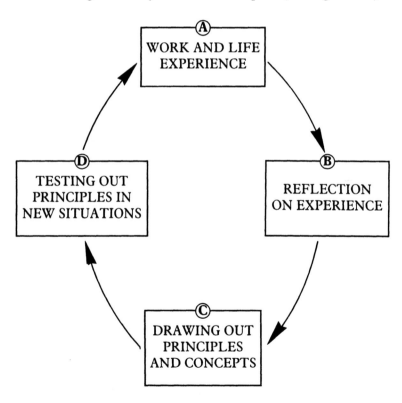

FIG. 1.1 Learning cycle, based on the ideas of David Kolb (1984) *Experiential Learning.*

that we reflect upon the experiences that we have just had. Thirdly, we draw out some concepts and some principles from this reflection. Finally, we test out the new concepts in new situations so that they become part of the ongoing experience, on which we shall continue to reflect, and so on in a never-ending circle or even spiral.

David Kolb does not use the words 'process', 'interaction' or 'change', but this is what he is talking about. It is noteworthy that he uses the word 'learning', and if you think about it, all these ideas come together and form a framework within which we can think about change and even learn to love it and welcome it. Learning is itself a process of change. Something is added to our perception and prepares us for the next impression, which will change our understanding yet more, however minutely. What David Kolb is talking about is the normal scientific approach, where observations are made and reflected upon to yield theories from which hypotheses are derived and tested out in action, creating new events and experiences.

Change is learning

The Kolb contribution is a significant one because it practically equates change and learning. When you learn, you change. When you change, you learn. A book on change is therefore also a book about learning.

Reg Revans of Action Learning fame would make a distinction with two little symbols L>C and C>L. If learning is represented by L and change represented by C then the first symbol means you are ahead in the game – you are learning faster than things change. The second can spell disaster, because things are changing faster than you are learning, so that you are behind in the race.

Nevertheless Revans is in harmony with Kolb in that his contribution of Action Learning is based on the concept that people learn more from reflecting, discussing and working together on real live issues than from being lectured at. They learn from each other and the learning is relevant, and even when the classroom is being used for input, it is important to provide plenty of scope for learning in this way.

A positive approach

These perceptions of what it is to be human can help us to take a positive approach to change and make it work to our advantage and to that of our enterprise. You are only really alive when you are changing. It is the essence of personal growth, it is the basis of relationships with other people, and without it there is no learning and no progress.

Yet even when we acknowledge all this, we are prone to resist change. We fear it, we avoid it and we sigh for the status quo.

Our aim in this book is to help you to generate for yourself an approach which will enable you to come to terms with change and go beyond, to enrich your life both personally and in the business sphere.

We shall invite you to think about changes in your personal life. We shall also share some of our own experiences to establish the enrichment that change brings to life, even though some of it is unwelcome at the time. We shall then work together to think about the great world around us, which is changing all the time and, in the changing, changes our personal lives.

In the rest of the book we shall apply the principles gained from looking inward and outward to the specific area of business and managerial life where, as Sir John Harvey-Jones has expressed it:

'. . . the task of industry is continuously, year on year, to make more and better things, using less of the world's resources. Management in particular is not about the preservation of the status quo; it is about maintaining the highest rate of change that the organisation and the people within it can stand.'

[13]

Chapter 2

THE PERSONAL EXPERIENCE OF CHANGE

The only way to think about change is to consider *your* change – the things you have experienced in *your* life where you have had to face up to change.

Managing change brings risk. We've decided to take some risks ourselves in order to get you, the reader, more closely involved in this book, even to the point of sharing authorship. It isn't normal for 'serious' books on management to include blank pages, but managing change requires converting the abnormal into the normal. We hope you find our risk worthwhile.

A section below is therefore left blank for you to pencil in your reflections, that is if you, like us, regard books as tools and therefore don't mind communicating with them pencil in hand and on the page. Or you might find it fun to get an exercise book and write down your experience in more extended form, thus creating the start of your autobiography, which after all is the story of your encounter with change.

Please take time out to do this before reading further. State how you felt as well as what happened. It will help to turn this book into one which author and reader jointly write. After it we will give you a selection of what we wrote in our exercise books. It might spark off some additional awareness of your own experiences of change.

[14]

My personal experiences of change

_____

_____

_____

_____

_____

_____

_____

_____

_____

_____

_____

_____

_____

_____

_____

_____

_____

_____

_____

_____

_____

_____

_____

_____

_____

_____

_____

_____

_____

_____

_____

_____

_____

_____

_____

_____

_____

_____

A few of Phil's personal experiences of change

Experience 1

Walked out of Sunday School aged five (because I didn't believe that Noah didn't have a compass). Discovered that although it was possible to challenge a well-established organisation, the strength that the organisation had by virtue of its position made it easy to exert pressure on me as an individual. There could have been a considerable cost for me to pay, but, because my parents supported me instead of the outraged Sunday School teacher who came to my house in hot pursuit, I learned another lesson. Understand your power base. Although you may not have much power yourself, you may have connections which can use power on your behalf.

The postscript to this story occurred about a year later when I tried to walk out of a school lesson (I couldn't see the relevance of William the Conqueror to my everyday life). I found that I had misread my power bases, and this time my parents did not support my actions. I learned two further lessons. The first was that situations which appeared identical to me did not necessarily appear the same to others. So I should not assume that what worked and was approved last time would work this time.

The second lesson was more complex. I thought that by walking out I would reduce the size of the class and so make things easier for the teacher. I assumed that I would find something else to do outside which would be useful – at least to me. But the act of walking out of the class was, to my amazement, interpreted as being disobedient and lazy. I learned that other people acted on their interpretations of what they thought to be important, not on the facts as I knew them. The notion of truth as something absolute took quite a hammering, and I have always had a great respect for other people's perceptions ever since.

Experience 2

At the age of 21 I was recruited by the United Nations Association (a voluntary aid organisation) which sent me to the Solomon Islands on the other side of the world to work in conditions and among people very different to those I had grown up with.

It was my first experience of culture shock, and it took me at least six months to begin to feel comfortable. I was dreadfully homesick, and despite being among charming and helpful people, felt disorientated and in some vague way generally incompetent at almost everything that was locally regarded as important.

I learned an immense number of detailed lessons about myself during this time, but one of the biggest lessons was the importance of the 'fit' between people's assumptions, skills and knowledge, and their environment. A fish out of water was pretty analogous to me out of my culture. But the story had a happy ending; after a year I felt very much at home, and after two years I did not want to return to the UK. I had learned that my ability to adapt to unknown and initially unliked situations was greater than I thought. I had tipped myself into a deep end, and had found life to be very difficult and uncomfortable, but to my surprise I learned first to cope, and later to enjoy, a set of circumstances from which I had originally wanted to escape.

Experience 3

In the previous example, although I wasn't happy at first, I always knew that I could leave if I really wanted to. I would have had to suffer a fair amount of personal ignominy and shame, but help, in the form of an air ticket, was available if I really wanted it. In the next example, however, I was the only person who could help me.

I had always been interested in flying, and I had saved up to put myself on a three-week intensive flying course. All had gone reasonably well, and I had been allowed to fly solo as preparation for taking my private pilot's examinations and air test. I was returning to the airfield after flying my first solo cross-country. On the way I had briefly been lost a couple of times, and so was tired and mentally drained. The airfield was by the sea, and, as I approached, a sea mist came in over the field. Under radio instructions I circled a few times to allow other aircraft to land, but as I continued to circle, my fuel reduced and my fear increased.

After what was probably quite a short time I found myself circling at 1200 feet above the hazy English countryside in a profound state of panic. Freezing up increases the danger, and the increased danger heightens the freeze. It had been a long time since I had felt this kind of total panic, and the realisation that my survival depended wholly on me added a kind of pressure that I had not experienced before. I realised how much I relied on my instincts, yet my instincts had gone adrift. I needed to be cool and mechanical and use logic to position and land the plane. I found I couldn't force myself to be cool, but when I started to get annoyed with myself, suddenly I found I could mentally push all that emotion to one side, and let the logical side of my brain take over to land the plane safely.

I had learned that even when things look very bad, there are other mental solutions that can help. I also realised that the danger was entirely self-created. Until I started to panic, I had been operating a perfectly safe machine in a perfectly safe way. The danger was in one sense an illusion. The voice that had been screaming 'I can't' so loudly in my head was my voice. In other circumstances I would have looked for outside assistance or tried to avoid the reasons for the fear. In this case that was not possible and I had to counter my own fear with my own anger, and it worked.

A few of Edgar's personal experiences of change

As I look back over 67 years of living, I realise how true it is that change is the essence of existence. I can think of change at the age of five from home to school and at seventeen from school to work; at nineteen from office to wartime farming; at twenty-nine to office again; of key changes in my activity in British Coal, as it is currently known, every seven or eight years; major changes, even traumatic ones, in family life; and then a new consultancy career in my sixties. It's all been a rich adventure; I sometimes say I've lived seven days every day, so that if I die at 100 I'll really have lived 700 years.

But this is a matter of attitude, of seeing each separate experience as a 'day' in its own right. Five minutes' conversation in a corridor or street can change a whole perspective – can even change your whole life. Five minutes' beauty as the spring sun slants through the Ashridge Forest gives a day's worth of joy – it changes how you perceive life that day. However, experience alone is not the keynote of change. Rather, as David

Kolb would put it, it is a matter of experience reflected on that gives change its meaning. So, like Phil, I've picked out three experiences.

Experience 1

The first was a two-part, but really ongoing, spiritual experience. I was brought up in a very small but earnest Christian Fundamentalist sect whose members' religion was central to their lives. They believed they alone had the truth, and indeed that only their particular sub-sect was really 'sound'. My childhood was a happy one, but I was brainwashed to accept this elitist position. I will never forget the thump of a package of books through my letterbox when I was twenty-one, which suggested that all the sub-sects of our denomination ought to be united, minor differences notwithstanding. I stayed up all night to devour these books and by morning light was convinced. The sheer joy of escape into mental freedom was exhilarating. I immediately put my new-found freedom into practical effect and was cast out of the 'strict' sub-sect into the 'lax' sub-sect. But I still drew the line at the rest of the Christian world.

Just over twenty years later I met a man who challenged all my spiritual presuppositions and turned my whole life upside down, and this culminated in my leaving the sect. This was the completion of freedom; my picture of God and human kind was revolutionised. I joined the human race and left the elite. At first, it felt daring, dangerous and slightly wicked, then it united me with all people who discover a little of the meaning of a love which is robust as well as caring.

What does this experience over a long period, with two crisis points, teach me about change? First it illustrates the fact that change has crisis points, moments of immediacy, but that the crisis points are usually the outcome of a steady incremental change: the crisis point occurs when what has been evolving is recognised as transforming the situation. Then there is in the case the sheer delicious moment when you query whether what you have always been taught to think really is binding, and you realise that there are other points of view. Change that you decide upon is liberating and creates a new world for you, but don't expect an easy ride. There is a price, but if change is toward something better and not simply away from something

[20]

old and tired – positive not negative – then it is worth the price. Life for me would have been poorer without a few experiences of challenging all that went before in favour of a new beginning. You can apply the lesson to any area of life where convictions run deep.

Experience 2

Another major change in my life was domestic: when I was 37, my son had a serious firework accident. He recovered, but a sad change was induced in my wife, who became schizophrenic and never in the remaining eighteen years of her life recovered full sanity. This required a total reappraisal of my life. I decided I would not allow the situation to become a total disaster. I would still live a full life and contribute to work, church and society to the full, while doing my best to ensure proper treatment for her. It was a response to a change which could have destroyed me and the family. It kept my sanity and in a strange way that of my three children. We have remained extremely close friends, we have a number of ventures and adventures going on collectively, and probably are so close because of the problems we had to face in those dark days that somehow did not seem so dark.

When I was 55, my wife one day put dinner on the table, sat down and died – a shock, but a happy release for her. In her madness she used to hear all the children of the world being abused and tortured. In her death she was buried in a corner of the cemetery near a children's playing field.

Perhaps the change lesson from this experience – again an ongoing change, sandwiched between two traumatic events (the accident and my wife's death) – is that when changes are imposed by circumstances outside your control, and are indeed most unwelcome, the human spirit is more resilient than you might suppose. On a day by day basis you can actually cope with situations about which, if you could have foreseen them, you might well have said – 'I can't bear the prospect: I shall go under'. But when it comes to it, you don't.

Experience 3

My third change experience is an ongoing one over the last twenty years. I never left Britain till I was 40, but since I was 46

I have travelled on fifty different airlines. Every year but one since then, I have spent several weeks in the USA, and it now feels like a second home. But more significantly, in terms of changed perceptions, I have had two exposures to very different cultures. I made twelve business trips to the Arab Middle East between 1975 and 1978, and I came to feel that Riyadh, for example, was one of my home towns. Then in 1986–7 I spent many months in the Indian sub-continent for Ashridge and the ILO, till it became my fourth home. Becoming sensitive to a radically different culture to the point where you feel unembarrassed about going, clothed in the national traditional dress, to meet the chairman of a state industry, means a deep inner change has occurred. One's humanity has become more all-embracing, and this is indeed the change that every manager who wants to become an international manager needs to experience within. The sense of difference has to go, while maintaining your own values: too often a sense of superiority lingers and the change is not complete. (Certain expatriates accused me of 'going native' for wearing local dress: they wanted to retain their difference.)

Life as change

We have taken the risk of sharing some of our personal autobiographies with you to enhance awareness of how much of life is about change; in fact you could say that life and change are synonymous. How you benefit from the experience of change depends on how much you reflect upon it. If you follow a Kolb-like approach, with its emphasis on reflecting on experiences, then change and learning also become synonymous. Indeed, life becomes a voyage of discovery and high adventure.

We felt it was worth looking at change from this highly personal angle as a means of inspiring a positive approach to change in that part of our lives which we call 'work', which is the main theme of this book. However, because work cannot be separated from the whole of life, it is good to reflect upon it in a personal context. In doing so a number of business considerations will have arisen, for you as well as for us.

[22]

However, before turning to the more specific business change issues, we will spend time looking at the theme of change in the whole world – the environment in which both our personal and business change experiences take place.

Chapter 3

GLOBAL CHANGE

Where does change come from? Some of it comes from within as a result of our own reflection, though even that can, in the end, be put down to our genes and our early upbringing. But most of it, particularly in business life, derives from what is going on out there in the world. Even if we or our organisations think we have initiated change, it will be because of circumstances in the world at large impacting on us. We have seen an opportunity or a threat, have taken action accordingly and have set in motion some change process.

The purpose of this chapter is to think together about change on a global scale and to see how an understanding of global change can help to make us effective change agents in our own bit of the world.

John Donne's famous comment on interdependence was never more relevant than in the 1990s. It is almost as if he foresaw European unification:

'No man is an iland, intire of itself; every man is a peece of the Continent, a part of the maine; if a clod be washed away by the Sea, Europe is the lesse, as well as if a Promonterie were, as well as if a Mannor of thy friends or of thine owne were; any man's death diminishes me, because I am involved in Mankinde; And never send to ask for whom the bell tolls; It tolls for thee.'

If people at work, from top manager to most junior employee, can think in this way, then they will not be surprised when change anywhere in the world impacts upon their organisation.

Unwelcome change is less likely to appear as a conspiracy by the bosses, and intelligent awareness of what's going on in the world will alert people to new possibilities, many of them beneficial.

We believe it is part of every manager's job to have this global mindset, so that he/she can help their staff to understand the reason for change and be more able to co-operate in turning it to advantage. It happens best where all employees can be shareholders, but even when they are not, they are stakeholders and their own interests are bound up with what happens to the organisation.

Future trends

A particularly significant part of this global perspective on change is gaining some sense of the trends unfolding, so that we may to some extent predict the future. Recent events, as we enter the last decade of the twentieth century, suggest that prediction is not a very reliable activity. Who at the beginning of the last decade could have predicted *glasnost* or *perestroika?* Who at the beginning of 1989 could have predicted that by the end of that year virtually the whole of Eastern Europe would be free from totalitarian rule, free to have a democratic system of government? Who would have guessed that the Berlin Wall would have been breached, or that the Soviet Union would be openly debating total restructuring?

Yet there are trends which can be observed, so that one can at least be aware of possibilities. This awareness enables us at least to make contingency plans. Thus, when major or even minor changes occur in the world scene, we can react in a way that will enhance the position of our organisation. We shall not entirely be taken by surprise. In some cases we can even take some steps before events unfold and thus get ahead of our competitors.

One way in which the change mindset of which we have spoken can be developed is to have a sense of what has been going on in the world during our own lifetime. This is not so that we can extrapolate from the present and recent past and have any certainties about the future, but rather so that we can have a sense of the instability of world affairs; that just as we have seen that change is of the essence of being human, so the world of human becomings is always in flux and moving onward, changing, developing. A sense of the history through which we ourselves have lived will help us to live in expectancy that the world in which we earn our living will go on changing. There will be fewer surprises and we shall be equipped to help those for whose work we have some responsibility to be less surprised by change and therefore less resistant to the changes we have to make because of global events.

The only difference between change in the last part of the twentieth century and change, say, seventy years ago is the rapidity with which it leaps upon us, where previously it tended to take us by stealth. Change happens faster, largely because of the tremendous acceleration of technological advance in the last quarter of the century, and there are no signs of the acceleration abating. Communications continue to cause the world to shrink, so that a wrangle in the South Pacific can immediately shake Wall Street, and revolutions are run from television studios.

Changes I have seen

To help gain a sense of the way in which change in the outside world impinges on the living of life and the running of business, we invite you to join in another co-operative exercise. Again we are leaving a section for you to write down, in any order, major changes in the world that you have seen in your lifetime which have had an impact on the way people live or society is run (or you may wish to use the exercise book again). Then we will offer our own list.

_____

_____

_____

_____

_____

Some changes we have seen in our lifetime

1 The universal move from horse-drawn vehicles to automobiles. (Edgar can remember the coalman and the greengrocer delivering by horse and cart when he was a small boy.)
2 Universal radio ownership, and also ownership of washing machines, vacuum cleaners, refrigerators and, latterly, deep freezes and microwave ovens.
3 Arrival of television and later of colour television.
4 Computers (and their reduction in size, so that the word processors on our desks are more powerful than the computers which filled a substantial building in 1958).
5 Supermarkets (well, pre-War we did have Woolworth's, the 3d and 6d store).
6 Introduction of electronic technology into almost every transaction and every article.
7 Motorways.
8 Good urban street lighting.
9 Universal electricity (in the 1930s a number of our relatives in the countryside had only oil lamps and cookers).
10 A population where many can afford foreign holidays.
11 Considerable expansion in the number who go to university (even though we have a long way to go on education).
12 Nuclear weapons and energy production.
13 Green awareness.
14 Wholefoods and organic farming become respectable.
15 Compact discs.
16 Extensive home ownership.
17 High-rise buildings.
18 Demise of steam engines and paddle steamers.
19 Fast track railways.
20 The emergence of Japan to foremost economic rank; its move from junk to quality.
21 The rise and demise of Stalin and Hitler and their -isms.
22 The development of the drug threat to society.
23 Sexual liberation.
24 AIDS.
25 The diminishing of formal religious observance.
26 The growth of sensitivity to world misfortunes (BandAid etc.).

27 The reduction in clerical work.
28 The industrialisation of developing countries.
29 Demographic problems.
30 Fear of energy resources running out.
31 1992, the growing integration of Europe.
32 1997, Hong Kong's return to Chinese control.
33 Artificial intelligence and expert systems.
34 The growth of militant Islam.
35 Miniaturisation.
36 Changes in the nature of work away from employee status.
37 The internationalisation of business companies.
38 Supersonic travel.

Review of changes

Your list of the changes you have seen during your lifetime and ours will probably include a lot of the same items. We can group them under the following headings:

- technological
- political
- social, including health and education
- organisational and economic.

These categories overlap and interlink and all have meant major changes in the way we run businesses and earn our living. If our lists span over half a century, what will even the next quarter century be like?

There just is no escaping change, and it seems to us that one of the key factors in being a successful manager is to be able to convey this sense of the normality and ubiquity of change to all employees. This will help to create a climate where change is actively sought and expected instead of being resisted.

Fracture lines

To help make sense of the changes we have seen in our lifetimes and the changes that we see emerging, the Welsh–Canadian professor Gareth Morgan has some stimulating insights in his book *Riding the Waves of Change* (Jossey Bass, 1988).

He stresses the importance of managers being able to read the environment in the trading village which the world is fast becoming. Managers have to 'tune into the future' and 'engage in perception gathering twenty-four hours a day'. He demonstrates that this exercise has grown in complexity. One display he presents of some forty-seven trends has over 'two thousand potential lines of direct interaction'. Thus it is a question not only of the speed of change, but also of the interrelationship of changes.

Morgan says it is not enough to extrapolate from what is happening at present. While picking up from the present, it is important to see the coming together of a number of forces, which are gathering momentum and have an ability to reshape the future of entire industries and their constituent organisations. He runs seminars in which he prepares managers for a constructive approach to change by inviting them to identify fracture lines in recent events and trends.

Fracture lines are breaks in continuity which may spring from specific events or groups of events, or from the introduction of new technologies or social perspectives. Thus the disaster at Chernobyl was one of those occurrences after which nothing would ever be quite the same. Every discussion of the development of nuclear sources of energy since that day has taken place in the shadow of the terrible day which spread its death-threatening influence over even the hills of Wales and Northern England. Other examples of fracture lines are the dramatic rise in the price of oil in 1973 in the wake of the Arab–Israeli war, the election of Gorbachev to the top role in the Soviet Union, the visit of Sadat to Jerusalem, the discovery of clear evidence for holes in the ozone layer over the two Poles, Tiananmen Square and the setback to the opening of China to Western co-operation, along with many others you can think of.

The key thought behind a fracture line is of a break with the past, an interruption in the continuity with the past. Sometimes what looks like a fracture line may turn out to be only an interruption to development. Thus it may be that Tiananmen Square may turn out to be an interruption but not a long-term diversion of the course of history. In addition, sometimes a number of smaller fracture lines may emerge from a previous one which paved the way for them. Thus the rise of Gorbachev is probably the real fracture line out of which many others have arisen. Any of the 1989 revolutions in Eastern Europe could have been looked at as fracture lines in their own right, and so they are for their own countries, but they would probably not have occurred without the predisposing event of Gorbachev's assumption of power in the Soviet Union.

This is not a question of delving deep into the philosophy of history. If you do that, everything is interconnected. You could probably trace the rise of Gorbachev back to the repudiation of Stalin by Khruschev and the failure of central planning as an economic tool over several decades, together with the growth in communications whereby it has been impossible to seal off countries from influences by music, television and other media. A whole range of causes merge together in the creation of history, so that it is difficult to say whether a Gorbachev creates new trends or is the expression of them. However, in popular speech we tend to simplify these issues and, for example, will speak of the rise of Gorbachev as *the* fracture line after which things would never be the same again. But this does not stop one from seeing subordinate fracture lines – more specific outcomes of major moments of transition.

It is important to read the newspapers and watch the news with this kind of mindset if you, as a manager, are going to spot the opportunities and threats implicit in what is happening globally. It is important whether you are the boss man or woman, or a middle manager who implements what others decide. Either way you do a better job if you understand your environment on a worldwide canvas.

By way of illustrating this approach, we made extracts during 1989, mainly from the *Financial Times*, of what we might call fracture trends in the fields of technology, environmental (green) issues, and international business. A break point or fracture line implies a definite event, but many of the headlines we gathered together were more in the way of pointers towards break points, evidence of a fracture process at work. It is for these that managers with a change mindset must watch out and relate to their own business. Whatever has happened since, these headlines still stand as examples of things which would alert the watchful manager.

The schedules for book publishing don't permit more recent ones, but it's the principle that matters, not the actual headlines. We have deliberately omitted most of the headlines about the Eastern European changes. They would take over – and anyway who can forget them? In the words of Wordsworth, 'Bliss was it in that dawn to be alive'.

These headlines are set out as an appendix to this chapter. You can ignore it for the moment if you wish and then come back to it later. Then you may like to mark up your newspaper with your own fracture trend headlines and get someone to collect them for you. You may in this way discover an opportunity to add value to your business or spot a threat which needs to be pre-empted. Do any of our headlines spark off in your mind any ideas for positive change which you could apply in your own circumstances?

Appendix: ECHOES OF THE FUTURE

Headlines created from a random supply of newspaper cuttings gathered in 1989 and early 1990

They are not dated nor in a particular order. They are listed to give an impression, the kind of impression an observant reader of the *Financial Times* might carry in his or her mind and apply in business. Sometimes we have included an explanatory note.

A *International business*

- Japanese investment in the UK. NEWCOMERS WHO ARE WELCOMED BUT FEARED.

- BIG COMPANIES COME TO THE AID OF SMALL COMPANIES IN KENYA.

- NEW FOUND SPENDING POWER IN A MORE DEMOCRATIC SOUTH KOREA BECKONS THE INVESTOR.

- JAPAN FEELS THE HEAT OF HOSTILITY IN THE US.

- THE DELORS REPORT: CHARTING A COURSE FOR EUROPEAN MONETARY UNION.

- US SERVICE SECTOR COMPANIES BOOST EMPLOYMENT IN DEVELOPING COUNTRIES. Arabic computerized script software, advertising, special software, leisure activities . . .

- CHINESE GAIN CONTROL OF NEW ZEALAND STEEL.

- CHEAP LABOUR AND MONEY DRAW INVESTORS TO THE PHILIPPINES.

- JAPAN'S GIFT HORSES ARE TROJAN HORSES. America glum about their future as a Japanese colony. Objections to the Japanese import controls – 'achieving by one-sided trade what it could not by war'.

- PAKISTAN CONFRONTS THE ECONOMIC CRISIS HIDDEN UNDER A PILE OF DEBT.

- BIG NEW OPPORTUNITY FOR SCOTCH WHISKY IN JAPAN.

- TRADING ON THE PROMISE OF PERESTROIKA.

- WEST GERMAN/SOVIET GROUP TO UPDATE INDIAN STEEL PLANT.

- MAZDA STUDYING PRODUCTION TIE UP WITH FORD OF EUROPE.

- LONG ROAD TO A SOVIET CONVERTIBLE CURRENCY.

- TURKEY AND AUSTRIA TO APPLY TO JOIN EC?

- FIRST SOVIET BUSINESS SCHOOL DUE TO OPEN IN OCTO-BER. Set up by the Italians.

- GLASNOST FOR SOVIET ISLAM AS MUFTI OF TASHKENT IS ELECTED.

- YUGOSLAVIA SET ON PATH TO MARKET ECONOMY.

- HOW TO BREAK THROUGH THE PSYCHOLOGICAL BRICK WALLS AND SET UP BUSINESSES IN W. GERMANY.

- INDONESIAN AIR INDUSTRY TAKES OFF. 'You cannot just look at aircraft manufactured, but at the workforce we have developed.'

- MAURITIUS – GDP GROWTH SIX PER CENT FOR LAST SIX YEARS. Problems of success.

- MUSLIMS IN THE SOVIET UNION – AN EXPLOSIVE MIX READY TO IGNITE.

- ALCATEL NEAR TO $1bn SOVIET DEAL. The Belgian subsidiary of Europe's largest telecommunication manufacturer will supply computerised telephone exchanges to the Soviet Union.

- MIDDLE EAST FEARS WAR OF PARCHED THROATS. Scarcity of river resources for Arabs and Israelis.

- ARGENTINE'S WINE EXPORT HOPES.

[33]

- TOUR OPERATORS CUT CAPACITY AS HOLIDAY BOOKINGS FALL STEEPLY.
- GENERAL MOTORS AND ISUZU TO INVEST 70m AT LUTON.
- THE KEY TO GLOBAL PERFORMANCE IS UNDERSTANDING LOCAL MARKETS. J.P. Morgan.
- LABELKING BREAKS INTO EUROPE. Small British adhesive label printing firm links with a Paris counterpart.
- NESTLÉ JOIN VENTURE TO MAKE KITKAT IN JAPAN.
- NISSAN AND TOYOTA ACCELERATE INTO THE LUXURY CLASS. Japan did it before with motorbikes.
- MERGER PLANNED BETWEEN BEECHAM AND SMITH KLINE BECKMAN. In search of the global prescription.
- CUMMINS ENGINE SACRIFICES PROFITS FOR MARKET SHARE. The world's largest diesel engine manufacturer by vast investment has defended its patch against the Japanese.
- NORWAY'S FRAGILE REVIVAL. Norway has recaptured its position as a leading maritime nation.
- JAPAN DISCOVERS MEXICO.
- HURDLES FACING FOREIGN INVESTORS IN PAKISTAN.
- GORBACHEV'S WHIZZ KIDS AT LONDON BUSINESS SCHOOL TO LEARN ABOUT CAPITALISM.
- INDIA WELCOMES FOREIGN INVESTMENT BUT FORM FILLING REMAINS A HEADACHE.
- THE ITALIAN ECONOMIC SUCCESS STORY OF THE 80s.
- SWITZERLAND OPENING UP.
- ROOM FOR BRITISH CONSULTANTS IN JAPAN.
- HUNGARY APPLIES TO JOIN THE COUNCIL OF EUROPE.
- END OF PINOCHET WINTER (Chilean economy expanding).
- HUNGARY DOES DEAL WITH AUSTRIAN BANK.
- AMERICAN VOTERS SEE JAPAN'S ECONOMIC STRENGTH GREATER THREAT THAN SOVIET MILITARY THREAT.
- SOVIET FARM OUTPUT DISAPPOINTS.
- GATT IN SEARCH OF LINE BETWEEN CHEAP EXPORTS AND DUMPINGS.
- JOINT VENTURES WITH EAST EUROPE: POSSIBLE 3300 IN 1989.
- NORWAY GETS A LIFT FROM NATURAL GAS PROSPECTS.

[34]

- VW PREPARED TO BACK DM5bn INVESTMENT IN EAST GERMAN CARS.
- FIAT ENDS YEAR WITH 29% RISE IN EARNINGS.
- WESTERN AUDITORS LOOK UP TO SET UP SHOPS IN SOVIET UNION.
- CZECHOSLOVAKIA ASKS TO JOIN OECD.
- PHILIPS IN HIGH DEFINITION TV ACCORD WITH PEKING.
- SANYO IN £75m SOVIET DEAL.
- JAPAN HELPS MOSCOW OPEN ITS WILD EAST.
- WORLD BANK SEEKS WAY OUT FOR MARGINALISED AFRICA.
- JAPANESE MANUFACTURING INDUSTRY RETOOLS AT RECORD RATE.
- UK CONSORTIUM BIDS FOR CZECH VEHICLE PLANT.
- SUZUKI SET TO ASSEMBLE SWIFT CARS IN HUNGARY.
- WORLD SHIPPING INDUSTRY WILL HAVE TO REPLACE 60% OF ITS FLEET.
- HEINZ EYE 30% STAKE IN WATERFORD WEDGWOOD.
- HITACHI TO BUILD CHIP PLANT IN WEST GERMANY.
- SKODA ENGINEERING (CZECHOSLOVAKIA) MAY OFFER STAKES TO WESTERN COMPANIES.

B British companies

- PRODUCT PROMOTION HAS TO RECOGNISE THE DIMINISHING APPEAL OF THE TRADITIONAL BRITISH FAMILY.
- IN SPITE OF MRS THATCHER, RED TAPE GOES ON GROWING.
- BODY SHOP CHOOSES GLASGOW SLUM AREA FOR ITS SOAP FACTORY RATHER THAN THE THIRD WORLD.
- MANUFACTURING INDUSTRY OUTPUT SET TO LEAD ECONOMIC GROWTH. (Report from Templeton College OXFORD.)
- EUROPE'S LARGEST URBAN DEVELOPMENT IN LONDON'S DOCKLANDS.
- INDUSTRIAL UNREST IN RESPONSE TO THE RESTRUCTURING OF LONDON UNDERGROUND.
- FORD'S ITALIAN BOSS IS FRENCH, A NORWEGIAN RUNS SPAIN, A BELGIAN RUNS DAGENHAM.

- HAMLEYS THE TOY PEOPLE SOLD TO US ENTREPRENEUR.

- HIGHER INTEREST RATES CUT CONSUMER SPENDING.

- Advertisement for BET, the service company: YOU LOOK AFTER THE CORE BUSINESS. WE'LL TAKE CARE OF THE CHORE BUSINESS.

- WOMEN – UNDEVELOPED SEGMENT OF THE LEISURE MARKET. (Henley Forecasting.)

- COURTAULD'S SUBSIDIARY TOLD TO THINK SMALL AND EXPENSIVE, NOT BIG AND CHEAP.

- INVESTMENT OPPORTUNITIES IN THE GARAGE BUSINESS.

- LABELS EXPORTED FROM HERNE HILL TO KUWAIT.

- CADBURY'S AND KODAK GO FOR TEAM DEVELOPMENT.

- UK DRINKS 200m CUPS OF TEA A DAY – BUT NO INNOVATION FOR 35 YEARS.

- WAR IN BRITAIN'S TANNERIES. SKIN IS BIG BUSINESS.

- RECORD UK CEMENT SALES IN 1989.

- SUCKERS FOR SMART PACKAGING – THEN WE THROW IT IN THE BIN.

- MARKETING TAKES A BACK SEAT IN INDUSTRY.

- GEC AND SIEMENS IN TALKS.

- BOARDS SHOULD HAVE MISSION STATEMENTS.

- NEW ICI PLANT USES NOVEL HEAT TRANSFER IN AMMONIA PRODUCTION.

- BRITAIN LEADS THE WORLD IN OVERSEAS TAKEOVERS (five times US, four times France, Canada and Japan).

- BTR IS STILL THE GRAND ACQUISITOR.

- HARD TIMES FOR FARMERS.

- MANAGER BUY-OUTS ON THE INCREASE.

- PUBS REMAIN THE CENTRE OF BRITISH SOCIAL LIFE.

- NFC FIND PRODUCT SPECIALISATION KEY TO SUCCESS.

- BP LIKELY TO SELL ITS MINERALS DIVISION TO RTZ. BACK TO BASICS.

- CADBURY'S RESHAPE THE EASTER EGG.

- CUSTOMER INFORMATION THE KEY TO COMPANY FUTURE.

- POWER GEN WILL TEST NEW FUEL (Orimulsion, 30% water 70% bitumen, to rival coal).
- BUILDING WORKERS ACCEPT 15% AWARD FOR MORE FLEXIBILITY AND TRAINING.
- LITTLEWOODS OFFER CAREER BREAKS OF UP TO FIVE YEARS TO EMPLOYEE MOTHERS.
- UNTANGLING FORD'S WEB OF WORKING PATTERNS.
- MARCONI, TURKEY SIGN £96m ORDER.
- ACCIDENTS CUT 1989 UK OIL OUTPUT BY 25.7%.
- BODY SHOP PLEASES WITH 31% RISE TO £5.3m PROFIT.
- TOYOTA TO START APPOINTING SENIOR STAFF FOR DERBY.
- NEED FOR LANGUAGE TRAINING IN BRITISH COMPANIES.
- RALEIGH HALTS PRODUCTION OF CHILD CYCLES.

C *Technology*

- EUROPE EMERGING AS FERTILE GROUND FOR BIOTECHNOLOGY.
- FRENCH PLAN POLLUTION-FREE COAL-FIRED POWER STATIONS.
- WEST GERMAN DIFFICULTIES WITH POLLUTION-FREE POWER STATIONS.
- ADVANCES IN VIDEO TELEPHONES.
- CONCRETE CRACKING CURED BY LIQUID NITROGEN.
- NORWAY DEVELOPS COMBINED WIND/DIESEL POWER PLANT.
- CASHLESS SHOPPING WITH THE NEW ON-LINE DIRECT DEBIT SYSTEM.
- SCRUPULOUS CLEANLINESS KEY TO JAPANESE SEMICONDUCTOR SUCCESS. (Workers must shower, refrain from scratching and walk in a way that does not stir up dust.)
- THE PAPERLESS OFFICE OUT BUT NEW METHODS OF PAPER MANAGEMENT IN.
- FAST GROWING TREES FOR ENVIRONMENT FRIENDLY COMBUSTION AT POWER STATIONS.
- ENERGY CAPTURED FROM TROPICAL WATERS. (Ocean Thermal Energy Conversion System.)

- JAPANESE ROBOTS THAT CAN HANDSEW.
- A LONG WAY TO GO FOR SUPERCONDUCTORS AT ROOM TEMPERATURE.
- JAMES GULLIVER SAYS THE ONLY WAY TO STAY IN BUSINESS IS ELECTRONIC SHOPPING.
- PEST CONTROL BY TINKERING WITH GENETICS.
- NEW SPEECH RECOGNITION SYSTEM TO CONTROL INDUSTRIAL PROCESSES DEVELOPED IN FRANCE.
- MEASURING THE BACTERIA IN MACHINE OILS: MIDLANDS BREAKTHROUGH!
- DEVON FIRM OVERTURNS 5000 YEARS OF TECHNOLOGY IN GOLD ASSAYING.
- BRITISH COAL HAS LOWEST SUBSIDIES IN EUROPE.
- THE AUTOMATIC VISITORS' BOOK AND BADGE DISPENSER.
- PEOPLE-WATCHING ESSENTIAL TO PRODUCT DEVELOPMENT.
- CHIPS THAT WORK SIDE BY SIDE INSTEAD OF IN A QUEUE. (Parallel processing eagerly awaited by the oil industry; seven minutes instead of seven hours.)
- WORRIED ABOUT CHOLESTEROL? FORGET DIET: THE DRUG COMPANIES HAVE PLANS.
- BT WILL BE 10% BASED ON OPTICAL FIBRE CABLE BY MID 1990s.
- THE SPREAD OF THE BAR CODE IN FACTORIES.
- GENETICALLY ENGINEERED BUGS TO COMBAT CANCER.
- WALSALL FIRM INVENT SAFETY LAMPHOLDER (thus getting rid of the last bare terminal danger).
- MACHINES AND HUMAN BRAINS STILL NEED TO WORK TOGETHER. THE NEED FOR HUMANISED TECHNOLOGY.
- CHIPS FASTER AND FASTER AND FASTER IN THE 1990s.
- TECHNOLOGY WIPES OFF THE GRAFFITI FROM LONDON WALLS. (Devon firm solves the problem of public defacing.)
- A PHONE IN YOUR POCKET WHEREVER YOU GO.
- BIGGER EFFORT IN IT FOR UK LTD COULD CUT TRADE DEFICIT. (Government support in highlighting profitable areas proposed.)
- MANUFACTURING SUCCESS BY REVERSING MASS PRODUCTION AND GOING FOR FLEXIBLE SPECIALISATION.
- IT REQUIRES HIGH QUALITY EDUCATION AND TRAINING.

[38]

- FIBRE OPTIC GRID REJECTED BY GOVERNMENT COMMISSION.
- SOLAR ENERGY FAST BECOMING A VIABLE ALTERNATIVE ENERGY SOURCE.
- PERKINS PRODUCE QUIETER DIESEL ENGINES.
- FOOD IRRADIATION SAFER THAN SALMONELLA INFECTION.
- COMPUTERS THAT GIVE EXPERT POWER WHICH CAN CUT DECISION TIME TO A FIFTIETH.
- FDA APPROVES DRUG FOR AIDS INFECTIONS.
- US TEAM ANNOUNCES DEVELOPMENT OF SUPERDRUG (Motorola and TRW).
- EXPERIMENT TO RECYCLE PLASTIC (Newcastle upon Tyne and Procter & Gamble).

D *The environment*

- WHOLE EARTH FOODS TAKES ADVANTAGE OF BRITAIN'S EATING REVOLUTION.
- WE MUST MAKE SURE THAT FUTURE GENERATIONS NOT ONLY EXIST BUT ENJOY THEIR EXISTENCE ON THIS PLANET (Prince Philip).
- NIKKI SECURITIES RECOMMENDS INVESTMENT IN THE GREENING OF BRITAIN WITH BET, JOHNSON MATTHEY, ICI AND SIMON ENGINEERING.
- RECHEM ENVIRONMENTAL SERVICES DOUBLES PROFITS FROM TOXIC WASTE DISPOSAL.
- BRITAIN'S DOLPHINS ON THE BRINK OF EXTINCTION.
- HELSINKI OZONE LAYER CONFERENCE SAYS UNEP IS ALL SHOW AND NO DOUGH.
- GOOD SENSE CAN HALVE CFC USE SAYS MONTREAL CONFERENCE.
- 25 YEARS AGO SCIENTISTS SAID CFCs WERE SAFE.
- HOW GREEN IS YOUR HOUSE?
- WAVE POWER BACK IN THE RUNNING.
- ENVIRONMENTAL UNIT TRUSTS' GROWING POPULARITY.
- DUTCH AIM TO SLASH POLLUTION BY 80% BY 2010.
- GREEN CONSENSUS GROWS IN EC.

- ONLY A FRACTION OF THE CHEMICALS AROUND THE HOUSE HAVE BEEN SAFELY TESTED.
- PURER WATER MAY WASH AWAY FARM PROFITS. (Fears generated by moves against nitrate pollution.)
- ALASKA'S ECONOMY HIT BY OIL SPILL.
- SWEDEN TAKES LEAD IN THE RISE OF GREEN CAPITALISM.
- RESTRICTIONS ON DUMPING HAVE CREATED OPENINGS FOR COMPANIES SPECIALIZING IN RECYCLING.
- BOOTS ADVERTISEMENT: LESS AIR SPRAY! MORE HAIR SPRAY!
- BOOMING WORLD MARKET FOR CLEAN-UP TECHNOLOGIES.
- BY 1992 ALL NEW VWs WILL HAVE CATALYTIC CONVERTERS.
- PRINCE CHARLES BANS AEROSOLS FROM KENSINGTON PALACE BUT PRINCESS DIANA'S HAIR LOOKS NO LESS PRETTY.
- THE SUCCESS OF BRITTANY'S TIDAL BARRIER.
- THE FUTURE OF THE REUSABLE COMPACT DATA DISK.
- HELPING THE THIRD WORLD TO AFFORD ENVIRONMENTAL CONCERN.
- CUTTING OUT FRIDGE LEAKS WILL REDUCE CFC DANGER.
- MCDONALDS SWITCH TO PENTANE.
- STIRRINGS OF HOPE IN THE BRAZILIAN FOREST.
- WORLD COURT TO ENFORCE INTERNATIONAL LAW ON THE ENVIRONMENT.
- PROPER MANAGEMENT COULD SAVE THE AMAZON FORESTS.
- BY 2000 MEXICO CITY POPULATION WILL BE 26 MILLION. THERE WILL BE 22 OTHER CITIES IN THE WORLD WITH MORE THAN 10 MILLION INHABITANTS. HALF THE WORLD WILL LIVE IN CITIES.
- BANGKOK'S ASTOUNDING REFUSE PROBLEM.
- MICROWAVE OVEN SALES FALL 30% IN VALUE AFTER SCARES.
- TEXACO HIT BY $355 ENVIRONMENT CHARGE.
- BMW TO BUILD CAR RE-CYCLE PLANT.

Chapter 4

FUTURE MINDSET

In the previous chapter we touched upon the way in which we can gain some sense of the way things are going and to some extent be ready for the future. We can see trends and be thinking of the possible shape of things to come, with a variety of options up our sleeves for meeting alternative futures. We shall be careful students of the unfolding of events, and we illustrated this activity by looking back over our own observation of change out there in the world. We also gave illustrations of how study of the press and media can give a feeling for the direction of events.

Future scenarios

Nevertheless, to see trends is not the same as being able to predict the future. Companies like Shell are famous for their work of developing scenarios for possible futures, so that when reality strikes, they have a plan to meet it. Thus the warming up of the Cold War had gone far enough by the early part of 1989 that one could reasonably be thinking how to seize opportunities as and when the Eastern European world was fully open to trade with the West. But no one could have predicted the rapidity with which the whole of Eastern Europe would change fundamentally. In our lives we can think of nothing so sensational in its unexpected speed and thorough overturning of the status quo. Nevertheless, by the time this book is on sale, there will doubtless be many aspects that we cannot at present hope to predict.

[41]

We can see possibilities. Often they are contradictory possibilities. The Soviet Union could move to political pluralism. It could break up under the pressure of nationalistic separatism, either peacefully and with sensible compromise, or via anarchy and even civil war. We can't know whether Gorbachev's amazing skill will continue to succeed. We could even find ourselves hoping that the revised status quo should go on a little longer to give the USSR and the rest of the world time to get its breath back. Some defence industry managers with whom we have talked find a dilemma in the 'breaking out of peace, all over the world'.

So business managers will be looking for the opportunities and threats in all the alternative scenarios. But they cannot predict the future.

Creating the future

Why then have we called this chapter 'Future mindset'? Our purpose is to get managers and workforces to think ahead in the sense of living in possible progressive futures and reflecting them back into the present. While recognising that we don't know what the future will be like, we should exercise an act of will to create new futures. This is a mental approach – a mindset – which projects itself into a changed and better future, and which resolves so to handle affairs that in one way or another, depending on inward and outward circumstances for its precise form, it will come to pass.

With this point of view we don't say 'We will do this'. Rather we place ourselves in the desired future and look back to now from that vantage point. We use the future perfect tense and say 'by 1999 we *will have* . . .' This tense takes us to then and sees now from there. Thus Professor Stan Davis called the American version of his book on the future of management *Future Perfect*. The British title is *2001 Management*, with the subtitle 'Managing the future now'.

Davis's theme is that too often in business life we are too preoccupied with managing the aftermath of what has happened in the past, in dealing with the consequences of events which have already happened. He goes on to add to the English language in his striking sentence: 'In the new economy, however, *we must learn to manage the beforemath, that is the consequence of events that have not yet occurred.*'

Managing the beforemath

When Peter Scudamore, British National Hunt jockey was nine, he wrote an essay at school about the future. He began with the words: 'I have been champion jockey for the past five seasons . . .' He didn't start with *now* and work forward. He started with *then* and worked backward. He knew what he wanted. So he grasped it – made it his own in the then present. Ever since, sustained by that vision, he has worked back to the present and then taken the necessary steps to turn his dream into reality.

You see a future event. It is real and you are certain that you and your organisation can bring it about. When that future arrives, it *will have* arrived because these steps *have been* taken. You look at what you have to do to get there from a more positive point of view. You treat the anticipated future as already in the past. This does away with the *if* we get there. Instead you are there and looking back at how you got there. It is a psychologically sound approach.

Looking back from the future

This future mindset is essential to the successful management of change. It engenders a confident approach, where change is welcomed as the only way to achieve anything worthwhile. It may seem a bit poetic and unrealistic; but try it at a meeting to discuss future plans. Get everyone to describe the future as what they *have done* to get to the future. Treat the meeting as a review of what *has been done*. Instead of debating what you *will* do, assume it has been done and remind each other of the debates which led to the decisions which yielded success. This will create some fun – serious fun – and take some of the heat out of the inevitable disagreements. It could create a new style of brainstorming. Like Peter Scudamore, you describe all your plans, proposals and visions in the past tense. You start your journey at the end. You create a self-fulfilling prophecy.

It need not be as absurd as at first sight it might seem. A board meeting to discuss the five-year plan can be anything but enlivening. It tends to look at all the possible obstacles and to vary the figures, trying to limit the constraints. It keeps saying: 'But *if* we did this . . .' It all too easily becomes timid and tentative.

Thus picture a special board meeting where the CEO has made it clear that this is a meeting unlike the usual ones, because everyone is going to be invited to let their hair down as a way of taking the first steps to creating a new future. The chief executive asks them all to write on their notepads the date. Though it is really 10 December 1990, he asks them to write down 10 December 1996. He then begins: 'It is December 1996. We have just secured the biggest order for pijongs ever known . . . There are lessons to be learnt from this. Let's just recap how we got here. You remember how in 1990 we invented the concept of pijongs and got everyone talking about them as a result of our mysterious advertising campaign. We didn't tell people what they were. In fact at the time we didn't know ourselves . . .'

After a little more in that style he asks others to recap the contributions they made to deciding what pijongs should be, and for everyone to pitch in with a retrospective rehearsal of the arguments for and against, and the alternatives which were proposed. He has already warned them to come prepared to talk about their proposals for new products, and he has told them to be ready for a new approach. At first they are embarrassed at the idea of starting in the future, but after a while they begin to see the value, and the flow of ideas expands. Creative imagination is kindled and anything becomes possible. The present no longer constricts.

It is rather like the quotation J.F. Kennedy made from George Bernard Shaw, who in turn took it from Aeschylus: 'Some people see things as they are and ask *why?* I dream dreams that never were and ask *why not?*'

The much used words 'vision' and 'mission' are relevant here. The following brief extracts from top managers with a future mindset illustrate the idea:

'While it is foolish to throw away the past, it is the future that we can affect. The ability to create and manage the future in the way that we wish is what differentiates the good manager from the bad . . . The engine of change is dissatisfaction with the present and the brakes of change are fear of the unknown and fear of the future . . . It has to be possible to dream and speak the unthinkable, for the only things that we do know is that we shall not know what tomorrow's world will be like. It will have changed more than even the most outrageous thinking is likely to encompass.' (John Harvey-Jones, *Making it Happen*, 1988.)

'It is up to the top executive to become a true leader, devoted to creating an environment in which employees can accept and execute their responsibilities with confidence and finesse. He must communicate with his employees, imparting the company's vision and listening to what they need to make that vision a reality. To succeed he can no longer be an isolated and autocratic decision maker. Instead, he must be a visionary, a strategist, an informer, a teacher and an inspirer.' (Jan Carlzon, *Moments of Truth*, 1987.)

'What a company needs is a "director of vision", whatever he or she is called. . . . A "director of vision" helps to shape the future . . . prevents corporate myopia and adds a "conceptual quality" to a board bothered about day to day worries. A "director of vision" can provide an element of magic. Companies shouldn't be afraid of that. He or she helps the company to aim for the products of the future: ones that meet future customer aspirations. The "director of vision . . . shapes the way you want to be and how to get there".' (From a conference of NEDO at Ashridge quoted by James Pilditch in *Winning Ways*, 1987.)

A prime task of the top leadership of an organization is to give the grand vision of the future. People at all levels can then break down this vision to arrive at their piece of the big picture. Indeed we need 'directors of vision' at all levels of an organisation. The more widely leadership and strategic thinking are

[45]

disseminated throughout an enterprise, the more integrated will its activity be.

As Davis puts it, the leaders of the future must lead 'from a place in time which assumes you are already there and that is determined even though it hasn't happened yet'. The former boss of ITT, Harold Geneen, expressed it as follows: 'You read a book from beginning to end. You run a business the opposite way. You start with the end, and then do everything you must to reach it.'

Of course, you may say that this is all right for the board, but less senior managers might find this approach less relevant to their functions. How could middle and junior managers, supervisors and people on the shop floor or out in the field apply it? We haven't disregarded this plea and will come to it later in Chapter 9. The future mindset applies at all levels and we will introduce some practical ways of establishing it, of helping everyone to be a change agent.

As Buck Rogers, formerly Corporate Marketing Vice-President of IBM, puts it: 'The people I enjoy working with most are those who believe that we can have an impact on the world around us' (*Getting the Best*, 1987).

Chapter 5

SOME KEY CHANGE THEMES

On the one hand, we have said that predicting the future is a tricky business. On the other, we have stressed the need to have a future perspective in order to introduce constructive change into the business of the enterprise. We have even considered how we can be projected into the future and look back from that position in order to approach change positively.

As we acknowledged in Chapter 3 on global change, one needs to have some broad awareness of whither the future is tending, a picture of future trends. That was the objective behind the appendix giving headlines from 1989, which suggested the direction things were taking in relation to British and international business, technology, and green or environmental issues.

This chapter picks up from recent literature some of the main threads of change which enable us to perceive an outline of the emerging future, so that we can use it to business advantage.

Four technological threads

We have already referred to the work of Stan Davis. We gained from him the concept of speaking in the future perfect tense – 'We *will have*' – and we have mentioned his book under its British title *2001 Management*. He makes a seminal contribution to thinking about future technology in a way which will yield business advantage.

His expertise on organisation structure led him on to an interest in physics, when he saw that both physics and management were concerned with 'the interrelationships of the parts of a whole'. He saw time, space and matter, which are fundamentals of physics, as equally fundamental to the shaping of tomorrow's business and organisation. He was seeing them as resources – time, space and matter – not as constraints, and he considered them as business resources from the customer's point of view.

Any time
The first dimension of physics which he links with business needs is time. As we respond to and persuade customers, they use our time until they decide to buy. Then, until we deliver, we are using theirs. We have to shorten the elapsed time between their decision and the fulfilment of their need. The customers want the product or service when they want it, not when the company deigns to provide it. They want it *any time*, and technology already provides many examples of meeting this need. There are thousands of services, from provision of spectacles to the development of your holiday snaps, where customer waiting time has been reduced from days and hours to minutes. Davis suggests that this should be seen as the beginning of a conceptual shift, a change toward getting as close as possible to *immediate* meeting of the customer's needs.

Immediately available response is growing in the banking industry, with the growth of instantaneous account debiting by automatic tellers at any time of day or night. Information has a time value, so that monitoring the production line in real time, or answering a business query immediately, benefits customer and provider. Computer-aided design in manufacture enables a rapid leap from design and development straight to production and consumption.

The technology is there. It is simply that managerial thinking hasn't caught up with it. This is where future mindset comes in, developing all the time to keep pace with the unfolding future. Those who provide goods and service in real time gain competitive edge over those who don't. There is no time lag between the identifying of a need and its fulfilment. This theme of the competitive edge of time has also been described by Peter Keen, in *Competing in Time*, as the role of telecommunications in facilitating immediacy and overcoming geography, as Davis's next point emphasises.

[48]

Any place

Customers want the product or service *where* they want it. They don't just want it where the supplier thinks it is convenient to hold it. They want it at *any place*. Already there are plenty of examples of this. We all carry around pocket calculators where once we would have had to go to the office to use a desk one. Month by month the number of people who carry the phone around with them is growing, and they no longer have to go to where the phone is. They practically wear it. Portable computers of the lap variety enable business people to do their spreadsheets on the plane; home entertainment systems are now designed for self-assembly, so that you no longer have to wait for the technician but within an hour of purchase you are enjoying the fruits of your investment, having taken it home in two or three boxes in the car. The customer, in effect, does part of what would previously have been done at the factory, as well as providing the transport. The manufacturing chain of goods and services ends in the hands of the consumers in their own physical space.

The ability to provide the product in any place is facilitated by the advance in electronics, whereby a million electronic components can be placed on a quarter of an inch square of smelted sand. The information carried by electrical impulses demolishes space as well as time and so enables the customer to enjoy both benefits. Davis cites four volumes of yellow page directories held on a 3.5 inch compact disc; then there is electronic home banking, and much more to come. No doubt all these innovations brought a lot of unwelcome change to those who preferred the status quo, but those with the future mindset prevailed.

These concepts of any time and any place also enter into the whole way a corporation organises itself. It is becoming less significant where you work. The number of home-workers is on the increase, with ultimate benefit to transport problems as the people work away on their computers. They still need human association and this is provided by the network. It is the ultimate in decentralisation, which is after all about place. As people work in networks, less dependent on space, so headquarters buildings are less inhabited and organisational hierarchies flattened. Middle managers find a new place between the producers and the customers, instead of between the senior managers and the supervisors.

No matter

Thirdly, the customers want the goods or service to be accompanied by intangible benefits associated with availability at the right time and place and to express values they require. For example, the man who came out over the Christmas holiday, diagnosed and corrected a very small fault which had put Edgar's central heating out of action, and put it right, wasn't selling him a spare part. He was selling peace of mind. That is the value he gives even when he's not needed, because he will come if he is and Edgar knows that.

Productivity is defined not in terms of tonnes of goods produced, but in value added per employee. People, as Theodore Leavitt pointed out long ago, don't really buy goods and services. They buy a value – something *they* value. The enterprise providing the value is able to share economies with the consumer by using as little matter as possible in the preparation of the goods or services. So automation and materials technology keep down the amount of processing and actual stuff which has to go into the provision. It will be produced more quickly and cheaply, and with less final bulk and weight. Davis encapsulates all this competitive advantage in his phrase 'no matter'.

'No matter' as a concept also includes the role of the disposable, though we have to watch its impact on the environment. But there are throwaway razors, diapers, cameras and pens. The idea of 'no matter' also covers the idea of the invisible purpose behind a sale. To perceive it opens up opportunities of lateral thinking and further beneficial change. The invisible purpose behind a drill is not the selling of drills as such, but rather to sell holes. If you use a laser drill, you are very much into the realm of 'no matter', for the laser is itself non-material and it produces holes which are by definition the absence of matter. This is all a question of tangible products fulfilling intangible needs. Ideas like this can transform a business. It is all about effectiveness of outcomes rather than efficiency of inputs. So the physical and the intellectual blend in the marriage of the change mindset and the future mindset.

Mass customisation

Finally Stan Davis gives us the paradoxical idea of 'mass customisation'. This expresses the idea of providing the customer with precisely what he or she requires, such as a garment to suit a bulky or a slender frame – something that is non-standard, yet can be produced on the same production line as the mass-produced goods of standard size, weight or other requirement. The technology now permits the non-standard to be produced on the standard line. Just a change of the computerised instructions and the trick is performed.

Gone the long wait while something is made to measure. The same technique can be used to provide cultural variations required in various parts of the world without setting up a special production line. Mass economy provides the benefit of scale; mass customisation allows for the differentiation and individualisation of requirements.

Future trends and change

The contribution of Stan Davis to our thought is valuable. He enables us to group the changes which have had the biggest impact on business, industry and society under types of technological development. Not so long ago you can imagine how some well-established businesses would have resisted such changes, no doubt thought of them as an unrealistic piece of futurology. Let us stick to what we know we are good at and so on.

The four concepts and the examples given illustrate what we have been saying about the need to approach the present from the standpoint of the future. That's how all these developments have occurred – so much so that we find it difficult to realise the amount of resistance they initially caused. Many of these developments are at a relatively early stage, so there is much more to follow. It is essential that managers who are going to have to cope with such changes see them as a part of their function to educate their workforces to understand the nature of the changes we can expect, of the world in which we live and the future we can create.

The future of work

We have already mentioned, in dealing with 'any place', the changes which are happening in the nature of work. Some of the best writing on this subject has been by Charles Handy in his books *The Future of Work* and the *Age of Unreason*. A proper understanding of the changes which are developing in working methods and hours, and in careers and employment patterns, can help people to be less anxious about the apparent insecurity caused by changing technology, methods and external market forces. As the pattern of work changes, lifetime work for one employer will become increasingly rare, and wider opportunities will emerge, though not without some hardship on the way.

Work is being affected by the way in which technology and social and economic change act together to create an information society, where information not only keeps us informed to an unparalleled degree, but also actually tells inanimate things what to do, thus drastically reducing the need for human beings to mind machines and perform basic processes. In his two books Professor Handy makes it clear that the days where everybody expected to work 47 hours for 47 weeks for 47 years are gone.

We are into the age of what Handy calls the 'shamrock organisation'. Answering to the three leaves of the shamrock, organisations are increasingly employing three categories of worker. There are the core employees who provide the permanent staff, performing the central activity; then there are the specialist functions increasingly carried out by contractors either as individuals or as companies; and, thirdly there are the casual and part-time workers who carry out the functions which are irregular, seasonal or variable. At different times of their lives, people may find different work styles suit them better. The parent with care of a child may prefer for a period to be part-time; a person retired from his or her main career as a core worker may prefer the freedom which contract work provides.

People may actually have a portfolio of approaches of work from which they invoke the element which suits the particular part of their life cycle. The portfolio may include wage work, fee work, home work (domestic, do-it-yourself, etc.), gift work (for charity or the community), and study work (self-education, hobbies). It's all work, and our identity as people does not depend on a particular full-time employment which people refer to when they ask us what we *do*.

The implications of all this are vast both for business and the individual. If society can get it right, it may mean more leisure and freedom. It will also have a bearing on the concept of a career for life, which is also creating problems for many companies where the career ladder has fewer rungs up which to climb, giving rise to the phenomenon known as 'the plateaued manager'. In fact, ladder climbing may go out of fashion with the reduction in the number of rungs, due to the removal of whole tracts of work through the impact of information and other technology. The challenge of the work itself will have to be the main motivator, and the cut and thrust of seeking promotion will be diminished, to the benefit perhaps of both company and individual.

Alongside these changes there are the problems of demographic change, where at certain levels there are too few of the age group from which you would expect the appropriate staff to come. Currently there is a shortage of school-leavers, and there is talk of having to raise the age of retirement contrary to recent trends, and to enhance the opportunities for women and ethnic minorities.

In addition, the types of employees required are undergoing radical change. Handy estimates that 70 per cent of all jobs in Western Europe will require mental rather than manual skills by the year 2000. Half of these brain workers will require higher education, which enough of them are certainly not getting in Britain or indeed in most countries.

Add these circumstances together and there is a skills shortage ahead, which will affect most companies and create a demand for further innovation to meet the challenge. Moreover, education and training will have the opportunity or even necessity to become growth industries.

The role of reward in companies will undergo change, and all sorts of ideas are being canvassed and linked with the tax system: zero income tax, social dividends, educational credits to be spent over a lifetime, a national income and ingenious ways of ensuring that the money is there from types of taxation which leave more choice and yet enhance the incentive to be entrepreneurial. Businesses and governments are going to have to study all these proposals with care, and the work of human resource management will undergo a radical reappraisal.

If all employees could understand these trends and regard them as a bandwagon to be jumped on rather than as a threat to be resisted, and if trade unions could see them as opportunities, then resistance to beneficial change would be diminished to the advantage of all. But even an insecure status quo is usually preferred to an unknown future. However, managers and the whole workforce are going to have to come to grips with the alternative ways of rewarding achievement, and at the same time paying for the needs of society. To understand these future scenarios *now* will make it possible to introduce change incrementally on a 'win–win' basis instead of by a destructive process of conflict.

In this whole area of employment the need for a change mindset which does not assume the permanence of the status quo, and of a future mindset which projects itself into the future and sees new possibilities, is going to be vital. There are revolutionary trends at work. It will be folly to ignore them.

The rise of the expert company

This is the title of a book by Edward Fiegenbaum and his associates, which provides another insight into the world of the future. It is the field of artificial intelligence, which is nothing to do with robots taking over and enslaving human beings.

This book is an account of how around the world such companies as IBM, Texas Instruments, Canon, Fujitsu and American Express are recording the knowledge and experience of their experts on advanced computers in a way which is already producing phenomenal savings of time and money. Professional work has been speeded up by a factor of 10 and in some cases as much as a factor of 40.

Examples are of customer orders for new equipment being turned automatically into detailed parts listings and transferred to the production line to implement immediate manufacture. Existing rule and procedure books and fault diagnostic guides are being produced and built into processes in such a way as to

[54]

minimise human search when things go wrong, and even then to give them the appropriate sequence of actions all ready to be 'switched on'. There are also applications in the medical field which could be of great help to general practitioners.

What the expert or specialist may do intuitively, will be done by less experienced or less specialised people, because they have computerised access to the mind of experts, whose time will have been well used by putting their very lives online.

It has to be recognised that the computerising of the experts' thinking is a very complex process, and that there is a long way to go before expert systems are really established, but the future mindset will see the potential and will prepare now for the changes implicit in the development, some of which may cancel out other problems, such as the demographic ones. In Japan a vast government-backed project is developing the next stage of computer activity, which will facilitate the expert system approach. It is called the Fifth Generation project. Fiegenbaum has written another book on the Fifth Generation, and says that these computers will make our present computers look like children's toys.

Not every idea with future promise turns out to be all that is expected, but we ignore the possibilities at our peril.

The green opportunities

There is currently a growth in awareness that the fears about the environment are not all bad news for commerce and industry. There are business opportunities as well as business threats. Large supermarket chains such as Tesco, Sainsbury's and Safeway's are recognising the need to offer wholefoods and organic produce to an increasing number of discriminating customers. The greenhouse effect, the danger of nitrates in our rivers, industrial pollution, acid rain, the ozone layer, all pose frightening problems, but they also provide the opportunity for competitive advantage, while at the same time helping to save the human race from its follies. There is bottom line profit to be gained from the growing awareness of what are called green issues.

Recent years have seen an enormous growth in that awareness.

Not a day passes without a major story in the media about oil slicks, the destruction of the Brazilian rain forest, dangers of pesticides, ozone-friendly inventions and tips for growing your own vegetables organically. Twenty years ago people who concerned themselves about these issues were regarded as rather cranky, as Edgar knows from his early days in the Soil Association. Now everyone is concerned. At first businesses were in danger of colliding with these 'cranks', who were regarded as a nuisance. Now, however, the prizes go to those businesses which take account of ecological issues ahead of their competitors.

These opportunities are well described by John Elkington's book *The Green Capitalists*. He tells stories of the way in which oil corporations have been willing to negotiate with governments such as that of Greenland and, by recognising the primacy of ecological concern, have gained the necessary permits to go ahead; and how corporations which learn from disaster or near disaster go on to redefine their dreams and ambitions and continue to advance, while those who ignore the dangers go out of business. Such companies as BP and Shell have at least as a matter of enlightened self-interest funded research into major ecological issues.

Elkington tells the story of how green supporters bought shares in Hoechst, the German chemical firm, in order to give themselves the opportunity of a platform at the annual general meeting. Such situations make companies recognise that they have to be ready to meet criticism effectively. For example, the Bayer company took Greenpeace and the Friends of the Earth to see the progress it was making in recycling sulphuric acid waste.

These and many other stories tell how companies reach a compromise with the green necessities, and more positive ones are about how to make profit out of being green. Thus the cost and waste from packaging materials and methods has in many industries been reduced in such a way that both the public and the manufacturer benefit, mainly by 'lightweighting', reducing the amount of energy and material used. Some companies are also recognising the sense of having environmentalists work with them, as in the case of David Bellamy's co-operation with the Nuclear Industry Radioactive Waste Executive (NIREX).

[56]

The story of Anita Roddick's Body Shop International is perhaps one of the most outstanding examples of a business built on ecological awareness. Producing natural products in cheap refillable containers makes both commercial and ecological sense. So do such investment trusts as Friends' Provident Stewardship Fund, which attracts investors who want their gains to be derived from sources which directly benefit humanity and who wish to avoid investing in tobacco, alcohol, armaments, oppressive governments, and earth-polluting activity. It is quite a successful fund, responding to a need which is strongly felt by a minority, and offering a market niche.

Chapter 6

CHANGES IN THE BUSINESS

We have seen the inherent nature of change. It is part of being a human being or a human becoming; it is implicit in being part of a human society or community. We have seen the association between change and learning and we have reflected on changes we have experienced in our personal lives, so that we can get used to the idea of having a change mindset which does not fear change, even when it endangers a status quo we value. Rather we go out to create change or to turn it to good effect when it intrudes in apparently unwelcome guise.

We have thought about the global changes that have occurred in our own lifetimes and the kind of future which is emerging and in which we shall have to earn our individual and collective livings. We added the idea of managing the present in the light of a vision of the future and we called that the future mindset – a subset of the change mindset.

Now we turn specifically to the application of these mindsets to the businesses in which we work. Businesses have their own fracture lines. We will follow a similar approach of getting you to become a co-author in the production of this book. Again we will leave a section for you to complete with *your* experiences of change in business life. Of course if you like to keep your books in pristine condition, then you may prefer to get out that exercise book and write down *your* change experiences at work. Don't include only the major changes; sometimes the small ones may have taught you a lot, in the spirit of the Kolb Learning Cycle, and small changes are often part of a sequence leading to major change. Be quite specific, too.

Then we will offer some of our own experiences and try to

pull together a catalogue of changes likely to be met to help us all identify them. Our own experience will include some quite small changes in terms of their relationship to the major issues which boards deal with. We want to see change in the small issues which affect the workforce and the junior managers and have a sense of the wider issues they may reflect.

_____

_____

_____

_____

_____

_____

_____

_____

_____

_____

_____

_____

_____

_____

_____

_____

Phil's changes at work

Change 1

The first change I want to describe is the introduction – you might say invasion – of mainframe computer technology in a large and sophisticated environment.

In the mid-1960s I worked briefly for Kodak during college vacations. As I was one of that new breed who had actually been taught computer studies, I was assigned to the new computer department to 'help out'. I found myself in a new, purpose-built office block. There were two computers there, an old EMIDEC with a revolving drum memory which occasionally used to catch fire if the lubricating oil got too hot, and the latest IBM360 with a wonderfully impressive display of flashing red lights.

A number of stories were being told about the computer department when I joined it. For instance, the whole install-ation was supposed to have replaced at least fifty clerical staff who had been previously needed by the finance department. Another story was that when the new IBM arrived, it didn't fit into the service lift and some of the front windows on the second floor of the building had to be removed to get the thing in. I don't know whether these and plenty of other stories like them were true or not, but it was certainly true that we in the computer department felt and behaved like an élite. The machines had to live in an air-conditioned environment. No one, not even the general manager of the whole building, was allowed in without permission from the operator on duty at the time – something to do with too many bodies imbalancing the humidity levels, it was said. But it gave the duty operator a lot of power.

I became quite familiar with the machines and their pro-grammes, and on occasions I stood in as an assistant operator. What impressed me was the way that my rudimentary knowledge of the machine and its operation appeared to grant me influence well above my actual role and position in the organisation. Quite senior managers came and asked for my advice and help, and appeared to take my word on matters to do with a lot of computer-related money. What surprised me was the apparent helplessness these managers showed in the face of this new technology. They assumed that my knowledge was absolute, and neither questioned it nor seemed at all interested in learning about the systems for themselves. It was almost as if at that time the computer had become a deity, and I and my computing colleagues had become priests.

Almost everything was done to satisfy it, and almost no argument that criticised it would be accepted. The cost-reduction arguments that I had heard used to justify the extension of computer resources really did not hold up. I never heard anyone say it out loud, but in headcount alone there were more than fifty people now working with the machine, i.e. those fifty clerical staff seemed to rematerialise in the shape of data entry operators, then of course there were the operators, programmers, analysts. Other costs must have occurred through the occasional computer error, which, being on a much grander scale than before, cost a lot more than a mere clerical slip.

However, I am not being critical of Kodak. I think the company was right to use computers as soon as they became commercially available. The company's managers saw a trend, and correctly decided that it was one that Kodak as a worldwide organisation had to be in step with. For me the important aspect was the way that able managers felt unable to engage with the new technology on a personal level. 'We leave that to the experts', was the normal approach. They failed to recognise that these technologies would have massive effects on every department in the company.

Change 2

The other major change that I witnessed at first hand was an organisation recognising the need to move from a product-centred philosophy to a market-oriented one.

In the late 1970s I joined British Transport Hotels to work in the area of management development. Although the organisation was linked to British Rail, it was a separate business and more or less its own profit centre. It had suffered in recent times from its success in previous years. It managed a series of high-class, stately hotels, run on traditional lines. The manager of each hotel was an hotelier in the classic sense of the word. He knew about wines, and was usually an expert in French cuisine (he would have spent two years of his seven years' training working in the kitchen of a famous French restaurant). He – it was always he – regarded his guests as personal friends, and it was his business to make each visitor feel totally at home, irrespective of the cost. The bill of course was picked up by the customer. But those were the days when most of the customers lived in an atmosphere of 'If you have to ask the price, you can't afford it'. The manager and his staff had a simple task – to provide the best and not worry about the cost.

For many years this formula worked very well. But then the hotel group seemed to hit a bad patch. Many directors said it was just bad luck; they would sit it out. So they didn't do much about it. For some time a lot of people convinced themselves that 'things would pick up again'. They had not realised that the market had changed, and that, although their customers still wanted good levels of comfort and hospitality, now they looked at the bill very carefully too. Value for money was clearly a need. The increasing numbers of business travellers and business conference organisers wanted different things from a hotel chain originally targeted at the leisured classes.

It took several years, and an almost complete change of senior management, before the group achieved its target of meeting the needs of particular markets. Along the way there was much heel-digging for some, and much frustration for others, who could see what needed to be done but hadn't the means to do it. Those of us engaged in bringing about the changes lived a life of continual presentation, confrontation and clarification. But probably the most important thing we did was to give other people support. We did the unthinkable, and tackled the unmentionable, and we encouraged others to do the same. A lot of mistakes were made, but in the end a major change had been achieved. Most of the hotels became profitable once more, and the majority of the staff in them became more energetic, more innovative, and more customer-oriented than ever before. What happened to the chain? It was broken up and sold off as the first in the government's privatisation programme. So even the change managers were changed!

Edgar's changes at work

Change 1

When I started in farming, we had to scythe an area round the field and then the reaping machine cut and bound the sheaves of wheat. We stood them up in stooks to stay dry, then we loaded them on to a trailer and built them into a stack. Two or three months later we had a steam threshing tackle in, put the corn in sacks, blew away the chaff and built a straw stack for use through the winter. In 1952 when I moved from farming, even the smallest farms were hiring combine harvesters! All in ten years! Of course, Canada and the USA with their vast acreages had been there for some time, but think of all the change implications there were in this period of ten years for British producers and importers of agricultural machinery and how many had their future mindset sufficiently developed to see the signs of the times.

Change 2

My first job after leaving farming was in the Stores Costing Department of the Midlands Electricity Board. In two large rooms some thirty-five people wielded pens on large ledgers representing the stores' movements at all the district offices, sub-offices and retail sales offices. Goods-received notes and stores-issue notes came in from each place, after they had been entered on bin cards at the point of origin. We laboriously entered the same information, financially expressed, into our ledgers – scores of them. Once a month we summarised it all and for-warded it into the financial accounts. Occasionally there would be comparisons between what our books said should be in stock and what actually was. Needless to say, they never agreed, and to find whether it was error or fraud was more costly than the value of the goods. Within ten years the whole system had gone and old-fashioned computers had reduced the staff and the work by 90 per cent. I remember the fears as rumours circulated that change was on the way and we might lose our jobs.

Change 3

When I joined the National Coal Board, my first job was in the Sales Accounting Department. Electronic computers were not in, but Hollerith Mechanical Tabulators were. They worked on the principle of something like knitting needles activating the calculation by hooking up together the relevant information. The installation had been a calamity, the invoices were weeks behind and the resultant cost to the Board was enormous. So about eighty people, I among them, were recruited to produce the invoices manually, just about the most boring job I have ever done, though I turned it into fun by having races with myself and with others. You could speed the process up enormously by various tricks (change!). Within five years it was all on the new first-generation computers, all that large staff had disappeared and some of us went on to good careers. (Another positive thought on change: would I be able to look back on a satisfying second career, on which my third career has been built – would I be writing this book if the Hollerith Machines had been properly prepared for and used effectively? I got where I am through the failure of a change, through unreal expectations from knitting needles.)

Change 4

I moved into marketing for a couple of years. I had a spell in pit control. There I saw how change overtakes you with stealth in some circumstances. It was the mid-1950s. Ever since the war, coal had been in short supply and the job of pit control was simply to share out the limited supplies as fairly as possible between the various wholesalers and industrial concerns. For two or three weeks I cheerfully did this. I attended a weekend course where we actually discussed the circumstances where we tell people to move to oil in order to ensure their energy supplies. Then I found that all of us with one or two pits under our control were building up stocks. We couldn't share the stuff out, because not enough people wanted it. Oil was winning. It was cheaper and plentiful. We supposed it was a temporary hiccup but we were in the middle of a crucial turning point. The evidence was before our eyes and it took us several months to realise that we were part of what Gareth Morgan nowadays calls a fracture line.

Change 5

Personal changes get interwoven with business needs, and we

make no apology for using them as illustrations. The whole point of this book is to help us grapple with change at all levels in a practical way. One winter the Asian flu hit Britain. The West Midlands divisional staff department was decimated. Out of thirty of us, only three remained at the moment when all the salary changes following a national negotiation had got to be implemented. The three of us spent the whole weekend and succeeded in doing the job; the outcome for me was a change into the wider work of human resource management.

Change 6
My next change was computers. In the early 1960s they were new and cumbersome, but sufficient to reduce clerical staffs by two-thirds in a fairly tight time frame. My job was to support the divisional chief staff officer on redundancy matters. I now lived change morning, noon and night, learnt some of the fears which technological change was creating and went round helping in the work of interviewing and finding openings for people no longer needed in their old jobs. It was remarkable how wastage and redeployment enabled us to ensure that no one finally became redundant. A number of people did well out of it – I among them: I joined the computer organisation and ran a substantial training operation for it.

Change 7
The following fifteen years in British Coal are well known to the British public: a continuing contraction of the industry, with uncertainty hanging over us all the time, two major strikes, and a number of administrative reorganisations. Certainly at the current time morale is in a pretty low state. Ultimate privatisation is likely. A few managers I have met recently see opportunity in this, but a lot of people have left and have found themselves new careers. However, I have met very few managers or workers who faced disaster as a result of all this change activity.

It is not what actually happens to you in the end that is significant, it is all the anxiety and rumour you experience that creates stress and unhappiness. I was fortunate. I am an optimist by nature and look for the opportunity, but I was still sufficiently affected by the stress at key moments that I could have done with the awareness I now have that ultimate disaster rarely strikes the enterprising individual in change situations. I also had to learn to accept personal change and persuade my family to accept it.

Categories of business change

Against the background of some personal experience of change, and to help you place your own change experiences into categories from which something can be learnt for the future, we now attempt to list some of the areas in which change arises and to bring some classification to bear.

However you classify change, the various headings you come up with are interrelated. We would suggest that the main headings under which you could probably place your own business change experiences are:

- Market changes
- Technological changes
- Organisational changes

Market changes
The market changes, customers want more or less of your goods or services, competitors have begun to get ahead in the race, government decisions have freed you or constrained you, world events have changed the nature of people's expectations, price mechanisms nationally or internationally have got out of kilter, new technology has superseded what your organisation was good at, political changes in other countries open up opportunities or close entry, and raw material shortages have arisen or their prices have shot up. All these create specific changes in your business, whatever it is.

Technological changes
The changes in the market place give rise to specific happenings in the company. If the signs are negative, there will be new urgency in the search for new products or the creation of new expectations from old ones. There will be the introduction of new technology, if it can be found, in order to re-establish price

advantage, quality pre-eminence or diversification into new products. There will be the decision to explore areas of the globe where you were not previously represented.

Organisational changes

These responses to the market place will affect the organisation. At worst there will be retrenchment, reduction in the number of employees, and reduction in the numbers of levels of management. The technology itself might require new styles of organisation, new skills and the upgrading of old ones. The number of operating sites may be reduced. People may find themselves performing totally new functions, which they may like or perhaps won't like, at least to start with. The only way to stay in business may be a merger or to be the subject of a takeover, friendly or hostile. With such ownership changes, other market, technological and organisational changes may follow. In some industries it is an endless cycle.

Understanding the relationships

If every manager and every member of the workforce could have some understanding of these relationships in the formula for change, then there would be some chance that acceptance would be easier. The above three paragraphs sound simple enough, but when you feel threatened by what is happening, you don't think rationally. Feeling takes over. It is all seen as some kind of conspiracy by employers, managers or governments to look after themselves. No doubt there can be elements of truth in this, but there is an inevitability about change: market expectations are not static, new technology is constantly being developed, and organisational responses are inevitable to these sequences. It is a simple matter of business evolution. Less secrecy and more openness, even at some risk, plus a major educational effort to get everyone in the company to expect change, and indeed to create it within their own spheres, would smooth the path of positive change. Chapter 9 will talk of ways to create this change mindset throughout the company.

Organisational life cycles

A useful way of being prepared to cope with business change lies in the concept of an organisational life cycle. The idea that the individual human life passes through a series of stages is at least as old as Shakespeare, with his 'Seven Ages of Man'. It has been popularised by Daniel Levinson in *The Seasons of a Man's Life* (1978) and by Edgar Schein in *Career Dynamics* (1978). We will in particular have read about and perhaps experienced mid-life or mid-career crises.

The organisational life cycle concept simply applies the same idea to the life of a business. Thus Valerie Stewart (1983) presents three phases:

- Pioneering
- Systemisation
- Integration

In the pioneering phase a few entrepreneurial people get together to develop a new product or service. They are bound to each other by mutual loyalty and the excitement of discovery and innovation. There is little formality, fast growth and the early appearance of results.

Then it gets a bit too big for this approach: guidelines and checklists are needed, but priorities are unclear, and confusion arises where the imaginative decisions of the earlier days continue to be made on the spur of the moment. So system has to be introduced: standards and consistency begin to matter, organisation charts and job descriptions come into the reckoning, and specialists are appointed. A bureaucracy has to be created. Clive Sinclair appears to have been reluctant to enter this phase.

In due course this second phase begins to wear its value out. The organisation becomes remote from the customer, there is too much paperwork and too many meetings, risk is discouraged, empire-building happens, and people play things by the book. So change has to be introduced again. The organisation may be decentralised, with autonomous cost or profit centres and a closer link with customers and suppliers. Some system remains, but team-working is developed and people are empowered so that decisions are made at the lowest possible level.

[69]

Larry Greiner has a similar picture of five phases and five crises which induce change:

Phase	*Crisis*
1 Growth through creativity	
	of leadership
2 Growth through direction	
	of autonomy
3 Growth through delegation	
	of control
4 Growth through co-ordination	
	of red tape
5 Growth through collaboration	
	of ?

In each case the crisis springs out of the accentuation of the previous phase. Phase 1 – everyone's doing their own thing and so leadership is needed. Phase 2 – when direction is too pronounced, people cry out for freedom and autonomy. Then when they get it (Phase 3), eventually it gets out of hand and controls are required, which in the course of Phase 4 turn to red tape. I suspect the fifth crisis is a renewed call for strong leadership.

One corporate entity may have divisions, functions or subsidiaries simultaneously at any or all of these phases. One skill is to match people's stages of life to the company phase: entrepreneurial people for Phase 1: methodical, systematic people for Phase 4, people-carers for Phase 5. Some might say this order represents a sequence – the young adventurer, the steady applier of experience, the mature recognition that it's all about people in the end.

Harry Woodward and Steve Buckholz in *Aftershock* (1987), like Valerie Stewart, have three phases:

1 Formative	– leader manager; inventing; learning risk-taking
2 Normative	– systems, procedures, measures, guidelines, formality
3 Integrative	– innovation, collaboration, new growth, freedom on the job, creativity

[70]

Valerie Stewart links her triad with the product life cycle, made famous by the Boston Consulting Group. Products move in the market place from

'Question marks'	–	high growth, low market share
to 'Stars'	–	high growth, high market share
to 'Cash cows'	–	low growth, high market share
to 'Dogs'	–	low growth, low market share.

The phase of company behaviour appropriate to these product stages will need to be recognised. 'Question mark' and 'Star' phases are favourable to the pioneer stage; 'Cash cow' phase requires a steady, systematic approach. If you have a 'Dog' on your hand, you need a pioneer in reverse, one who will risk all to cut your losses.

Where does your company or organisation lie on these life-cycle continua? Or what parts of your organisation lie where? It will help adaptation to change to know where you stand, and understanding 'the global scene' and having a 'future mindset' will help you to find out where you are and whither you are headed.

Chapter 7

TRIGGERS FOR CHANGE

In our last chapter we looked at the broad background to change in business. We saw that change was expressed through three main areas: the market itself, the technology to meet market demand competitively, the organisation of resources and the enterprise to achieve success. We also considered the tendency of companies to follow a pattern of similar life cycles. The stage in the life cycle could affect the nature of the changes which might be expected.

The Ashridge Change Data Base

We now want to fill out the picture by examples of specific changes in business and industry drawn from the Ashridge Management Research Group's 'Change Data Base'. This data base was created from an examination of published and un-published information about some 200 companies in the UK, Continental Europe and the United States of America. A detailed analysis was published in *Triggers for Change* (Wille, 1989), originally commissioned by Ashridge Management Development Services Ltd, and also used on the Ashridge Management College programme 'Making Change Work'.

There were public and private organisations in fields ranging through engineering; leisure; electronics; computers; heavy equipment; shipbuilding; financial services; food, drink and tobacco; transport; airlines; energy; travel; local government; central government; retailing; oil; glass; automobiles; con-struction and building materials; chemicals; pharmaceuticals; textiles; clothing; police; and architects.

The organisations tended to be at the larger end because the information was more readily available, though this is not to denigrate the significance of the smaller businesses, which employ a large proportion of the population in the countries under review. We reproduce information about these organisations in Tables 7.1 and 7.2, by permission of Ashridge Management Research Group (AMRG), and then go on to draw specific illustrations of business changes from the detail of the data base in ways that we hope you will be able to relate to.

Table 7.1 is concerned with the causes of change – what triggered action. Table 7.2 presents a broad classification of the types of change which responded to these triggers. These two categories of analysis are not mutually exclusive. Thus the arrival of a new chief executive officer (CEO) may be both a response to triggers and a trigger for further change.

Similarly, a technological opportunity may trigger changes in work practices, and these in turn will trigger need for training or new methods of reward. Change is interconnected and never-ending. If you change one part of the system, there will be a knock-on effect, and it is very important to be aware of this. Otherwise a primary change will give rise to unexpected secondary ones which may invalidate the hoped-for benefits.

Table 7.1 *Triggers for change*

	No. of companies = 178
	%
Financial losses	24
Drop in profits	
Increased competition	23
Loss of market share	
Industry in recession	6
New chief executive officer	16
Proactive	23
(opportunities or threats foreseen)	
Technological development	8
Staff utilisation	2

Note: There is frequently more than one trigger for change in any one organisation.

[73]

Table 7.2   *Types of change*

		No. of companies = 178
		%
A	ORGANISATIONAL	
	Culture	30
	Organisational structure	44
B	MARKET-LED ISSUES	
	Customer market orientation	30
	New products	8
	Reduction to core	10
	Internationalise	14
	Quality emphasis	11
C	PEOPLE ISSUES	
	Communications/participation	23
	People matters	10
	Reward development	6
	Emphasis on training and development	25
	New work practices	15
	Teams/groups/task forces	8
D	TECHNOLOGY	
	Technology	16
E	ENTREPRENEURIAL–CREATIVE	
	Innovation	4
	Entrepreneurship	5
F	ECONOMICS	
	Costing cutting	6
	Staff reductions	9
	Productivity	7

Note: There is frequently more than one type of change in any one organisation.

Crisis change

Taking the results of the Ashridge Research as a whole, we see that change was often triggered by the need to meet danger or to avoid impending disaster. So about a quarter of the triggers for change which emerged in the research related to change initiated in order to cope with drops in profits, sluggishness of growth or downright financial losses (see the first three items in

Table 7.1). Thus ICI was shocked into action by the first quarterly loss in its history; ICL reacted to a threat to its continued existence; Massey–Ferguson responded to a world slump in its industry; Assuag–SSIH–Swatch introduced change to stop its market share evaporating; Schneider staunched the process of 'bleeding to death'; and even IBM had to introduce changes when faced with an earnings slump, though it would claim that change is its business anyway.

It is not surprising that change will often stem from a threat to financial results. After all, financial disaster means that in the end there will be no company. If there is openness in the company, the workforce can at least understand changes of this nature. Often, however, a normally secretive company will create suspicion if it suddenly becomes open because of crisis. Workers feel it's an excuse to bulldoze changes to 'line the shareholders' pockets'. This suggests that openness is essential in a company where change is a way of life. Of course, too much openness may also depress share values.

Proactive change

A quarter of the companies in Table 7.1 report proactive changes. The trigger was someone's perception of the shape of things to come, an opportunity or a threat. Action was being suggested while there was time. The perception was proactive and the response was proactive. Corrective action was being taken before a market decline or before technology became obsolete. Positive action was being taken to seize competitive advantage before someone else did.

Thus TSB, an organisation created out of a number of people's banks, saw that ordinary people were becoming more prosperous and were going to need a wider range of financial services. Accordingly it took steps towards such a future, and began to 'manage the consequences of events which had not yet occurred' (Davis, 1988).

Similarly, the Prudential Corporation in the UK expanded from insurance to a wider range of financial services. So did London Life and the German Bank TuB. Similarly in the US, banks were deregulated and were able to introduce changes to widen their scope.

[75]

Chief executive officer (CEO) and change

In about 16 per cent of the reports analysed, the advent of a new CEO was identified as associated with substantial change (see Table 7.1). Although sometimes a new CEO might simply succeed one who had retired in a normal way, most often the new CEOs were brought in for the very purpose of handling difficulty. The advent of the CEO and the changes introduced go together as part of the package to deal with crisis, so that many of the actions taken by CEOs appear in Table 7.2 as types of change, illustrating further the indissolubility of triggers and types of change. Strong leadership from the top certainly is fundamental, and it is appropriate that this major responsibility of the woman or man at the top should be acknowledged. However, it must never be forgotten that the top person can only achieve success with the support of the rest of the employees, managerial and otherwise. Part of the skill of the CEO is to mobilise this support.

Nevertheless we found that our source material often read as if the top person was solely responsible for the changes undertaken. Obviously we need some balance here. Often some steps had already been taken on which the CEO had been able to build and in any event, as Ben Thompson-McCausland has said:

'Significant corporate change cannot be achieved by one man alone, and even the active support of all the managers in a company is no more than the first crucial step. It means touching the hearts and minds of everybody working in an organisation, because it is in those hearts that the organisation actually exists. It does not exist in balance sheets, buildings or computers.'

Leaders are not found only at the top. There are many leaders in middle management and on the shop floor, without whom those at the top could not achieve their results. If their preoccupations are sometimes with relatively small matters, their successes remind us that it is the little things that often make a big difference.

There are many examples of CEOs who provided this inspiration and communicated well with all their staff. They were able to project a vision, a sense of direction and an energy to get results. Jan Carlzon of SAS and Sir John Harvey-Jones of ICI, from both of whom we have quoted, come to mind. Sir Colin Marshall of British Airways (BA) and Ian Hannah of Thistle Hotels attended all the seminars run for staff of all levels. Sandy Sigoloff, of the American firm Wickes, and Lee Iacocca of Chrysler stimulated people even when giving them bad news. Marshall at BA showed his commitment to serving the customer by going so far as to clean out some of the toilets, in a blaze of publicity, as a signal to everyone.

Mission statements

Top managers have used the development of 'mission statements' as significant contributions to the promotion of proactive change, often involving groups of managers and other employees in the work. Mission statements give the *why* that inspires every *how*. Thus Sir John Harvey-Jones gave expression to the purpose of ICI: 'to create a 21st century company – *now*' (foreshadowing Stan Davis's 'managing the consequences of events which haven't yet occurred'). His concept was that of 'institutionalising change by reweaving the firm's social fabric'. Of course, these are high-sounding phrases and may be treated with cynicism by some. However, they do focus attention, and when worked out in a practical way and turned into action plans that affect the bottom line, such slogans, signals, and mission statements can help to create a culture for change. One of the objects of this book is to help to create response to such messages and a willingness to work for a new climate, again expressed by Sir John Harvey-Jones as the injection into the business of 'a sense of pride, confidence, dynamism, excitement and fun'.

For Ian Hannah, MD of Thistle Hotels, the key mission in the first half of the 1980s was to make 'the standard of service match the quality of the physical facilities'. This, at first hearing, may sound rather general, but as it worked into the corporate consciousness, it was something everyone could turn into practical action *today*. They could see the improved décor and be challenged to act in tune with it. Old attitudes would appear outmoded.

Sir John Read gave TSB the mission to be 'number one financial firm in the 1990s' – an aim which knew no limits; one in which progress could be measured and which would instil the change mindset.

Jan Carlzon, of SAS, is well-known for the way in which he fired the whole airline with the idea of daily 'moments of truth', as employees at any level came face to face with the customers who were the real *raison d'être* for the company's existence. A simple phrase – moments of truth – helped change to penetrate the whole organisation. A leader was able to encapsulate a whole philosophy in a phrase which became a catchword on everybody's lips, inspiring them moment by moment. Words so used are not to be belittled: as with Churchill's in the Second World War, they are tools for winning battles in their own right – the battle for hearts and minds mobilised against inertia and self-doubt. Managers at any level who have imagination and a way with words can employ them with their own teams. You don't have to wait for the top man. You can even have a fun competition for such a slogan for your own work group.

Other examples of expressing new missions are found in the Prudential Corporation (UK), to change its self-image from one of staidness to drive. Rank–Zerox identified its mission as 'everything to do with office documents'. Dayton Hudson, the American department store, defined its mission as to be 'the purchasing agent for our customers' – simple to understand by mobilising attention on the quality of suppliers' provision. The emphasis on customers is here on finding and getting what they want. One can well imagine the practical day to day changes involved in such a reorientation.

Roger Smith reshaped General Motors by 'demonstrating to fellow Americans in industry that timidity is not the answer. 'Retrenchment is no solution. At GM we say "go for it. And we have. The vision is paying off".'

Personal styles

Top people do not conform to one pattern. Some are charismatic, some even flamboyant. Most of those we have just mentioned tended that way, but there are others like Mac Booth of Polaroid, Sir Peter Walters of BP and Roger Smith of General Motors who employed their quieter style to shift gear in whole organisations. Sometimes, too, CEOs were changed, not because they were not effective leaders, but because of the need to match strengths to situations. Thus Robb Wilmot in ICL provided strategic vision, whereas his successor Peter Bonfield was adept at implementation.

Another point to be noted is that effective CEOs do not have to be 'nice guys'. They have to be resolute and tough. Some manage to do this in an affable manner. Others may appear almost brutal. Whatever the personal style, unpalatable decisions have to be reached and top people need the resilience to make them and take unpopularity and opposition in their stride. Some CEOs, like Ken Olsen of DEC, seemed to be able to work in either style, depending on the need of the moment. He reshaped DEC by 'teasing, goading and teaching employees, sermonising and by remorselessly pillorying those who stood in his way'. Yet he was also accused of 'indirection' which caused the reorganisation to take five years. Carlo Benedetti engaged in drastic surgery when he removed almost the whole first-line management at Olivetti. Sigoloff at Wickes sacked the whole of his finance department.

Organisational change

Most CEOs seeking to improve results do something about the organisational structure and culture of their enterprise. Thus it is not surprising that in Table 7.2 organisational structure and cultural issues together head the types of change recorded in the Ashridge data. Organisation is a matter of structuring the way in which resources are brought and kept together in order to achieve objectives. These resources include people, places, money, materials, machines and so on, for a number of these may actually be needed in any particular type of change.

Nevertheless the emphasis in organisation restructuring and culture modification is not on the resources themselves, e.g. not on people as individuals, but on the way in which they are interlinked and mobilised, where the resources are positioned, how co-ordination is ensured and the pattern of share beliefs and values created to give cohesion and provide the basis of behaviour in the enterprise (see our definition of management, p. 6).

We would expect most changes to have some implications for the way in which resources and relationships are organised. Whether corrective action is being taken or opportunities are being seized, the organisational change will make a difference to the immediacy of reaction and speed of decision-making, information-sharing, communications and policy-implementation.

The CEO of Jacobs-Suchard declared that organisational stability was the biggest barrier to renewal, the German Bank TuB moved from its former aristocratic approach, and Alvin Toffler showed AT&T in America the need to be ruthless in reviewing its basic premises if it was to avoid becoming part of a museum of corporate dinosaurs. The culture changes brought about by reorganising are the most difficult to handle, and the ones that take longest. They have to overcome the inhibitions of a whole corporate life history, and they are likely to meet emotional resistance.

Organisational restructuring has contributed most to effective change where it has been something more than redrawing organisation charts. Sir Peter Walters took BP from a hierarchical structure to what he called 'a solar system of operating units circling round the central sun', with headquarters as the centre of a dynamic system rather than the top of a rigid pyramid. Line managers were made responsible for achieving financial targets implicit in change. A matrix structure was introduced to enable managers of subsidiaries to look after the general interests, as well as those which gave local advantage.

Decentralisation of detailed responsibility to operating units, with main board retaining only the broadest direction crops up repeatedly as the route to successful change. Layers of hierarchy reduced, a move from commodity to value added products, acquisitions, and international expansions are exemplified in companies such as ICI; JC Bamford Excavators (JCB) (where reducing levels of management released the energies of people who knew the business in depth and detail); ASEA (where even before its merger with BBC Brown Boveri restructuring had eliminated 4000 jobs, but paved the way for the subsequent creation of 6000 new jobs); Electrolux (described at one stage by CEO Anders Scharp as 'hundreds of independent villages', though latterly more a matter of inter-dependent networks, but either way, places where people and through them the company can grow); Jacobs-Suchard (whose frequent changes at the top encourage managers to maintain a business overview, because they never know when their specific functions may change, yet the requirement remains to contribute to total corporate effectiveness); and SAS (where managers of profit centres were expected to act in an entrepreneurial manner). It is interesting that the other side of the coin is manifest in 3M, where autonomy had gone too far, with forty fragmented divisions. The benefits of creative freedom had to be set against strategic co-ordination in fast-moving high-technology markets and a measure of centralisation was reintroduced.

Emotional resistance to change emerged in a number of the stories in the Ashridge data base. It was no easy job to mobilise Swatch to adopt Japanese methods of making inexpensive watches. Fagor, the Spanish Co-operative, must have found it emotionally hard to 'go corporate'. Organisational change has to take into account the something beyond reason alone embedded in culture and tradition.

Nevertheless the restructuring of organisations will have to be essentially rational – and it will move in different directions, depending on need. This is particularly true of the issue 'centralise versus decentralise'. JCB Excavators did both for different parts of the organisation.

Many organisations engaged in major organisational and cultural change found it useful to bring in reputable outside consultants. It helped in thinking the problems through; a fresh and impartial mind can shed new light on a situation. Moreover, the views of outsiders can carry weight as they have no axe to grind and acceptance of difficult decisions may be achieved through their good offices. Of the 178 companies in the Ashridge data base, some forty mentioned the use of consultants, and there were, no doubt, many others who used them but made no mention of the fact.

The market, quality and change

High in Table 7.2, listing the types of change recorded in the data base, stands the move to a market-led approach. This is a commercial as well as a cultural issue. It also links with the developing of new products to meet market demand, with emphasis on quality and service, with internationalisation, and with the alternatives of diversification on the one hand and going back to the core business on the other.

So we have the ICI Agricultural Division creating a link between marketing and every department, SAS spending lavishly on marketing when the financial situation was grim, and the banks and insurance companies which expanded into financial services setting up marketing activity as the key to success. As part of the market-led philosophy, a new emphasis on quality, feeding on the work of Deming, of Juran and of Crosby, is a key change element in many companies.

Quality became the key factor in the changes which put Jaguar back on the map. The British Airways change programme was all about customer service becoming the consuming concern of every employee. It was about quality of service to win markets. SAS had already found success in this approach. The French credit and leasing firm, UFB-Locabail, developed a change programme which permeated the organisation with quality circles. Continent, the French Hypermarket chain, did the same.

People and change

Market-led change and the concern with quality again demonstrates the primacy of people when undertaking change. It has become a truism to say that people are a company's most valuable resource, but effective change agents really mean it. Every type of change so far mentioned depends for its success on people, so that it is not surprising that British Airways launched a campaign for effective service with the slogan 'Putting People First'. Similarly, the search for quality in the two French firms mentioned above was rooted in people; a major purpose of their quality circles was to give their employees a sense of owning the enterprise and to create an inner compulsion to provide quality.

People just have to be central to all change activity. The plain fact is that while machines, materials, and vehicles have change imposed upon them, they will not answer back. They are passive recipients of change. But people do and will answer back, and none of the changes brought about in relation to things and material can happen without people playing their part.

So the Ashridge data base has a lot to tell of how people's hearts and minds were won, or how they were alienated by lack of clear communication. Resistance to change is natural and cannot be bulldozed out of the way. Understanding this is crucial to successful change.

Thus communication, participation, training and development, new working practices, and team development feature prominently in the types of change taking place in organisations. Reward development is not mentioned so frequently in our sources, but it is often associated with the whole package of change, even when not singled out. The really effective change agent empowers people. Everyone in the company is helped to realise that they can make a difference, that they have more power than they think they have. Quality circles, improvement groups, and decentralisation can all help people to grow.

Training and development

One gets some idea of the sincerity of a company's awareness of the value of its people by the attitude it takes to their training and development, even in times of austerity. The wise company will be like the farmer who, in times of near famine, still has to sow scarce seed if there is to be a harvest next year. Examples of this are seen in the mammoth investment made by ICL in training (24 per cent of operating profits in 1986) and in the empowering development programme laid on by the North American aircraft component firm, United Technologies.

There are many examples of the empowering role of communication, participation and personal and collective development (often under-described as training) in pursuing change through people. Particularly noticeable in this regard is the use of seminars/workshops all the way 'down' an organisation to cascade the vision from the top and integrate it with visions at all levels from people often nearer to the places which make things happen on a daily basis.

British Airways brought in 'Time Manager International' to involve all employees in their customer car programme – 'Putting People First'. Courage, the brewers, held consultative workshops throughout the period of building a new brewery, to hammer out the problem of how to use new technology without robbing work of its interest and skill. The brewery staff still exercise the skill that determines the quality of the beer. The ICI Agricultural Division set up a 'marketing initiative' to focus on the customer. The whole corporation used seminars to inject into the business a 'sense of pride, confidence, dynamism, excitement and fun'. ICI Fibres ran brainstorming workshops to extend their vision. London Life, before its merger, was changed by the extensive management development and training programme set up by Ben Thompson-McCausland in pursuit of 'change through shared values'. He introduced an experimental approach to the human mind, proactively and negatively, rationally and emotionally.

Involvement

Rank–Xerox based its corporate development on a similar concept. It viewed a corporation as having an organic life. It saw it as a living entity which grows and learns and breathes and thinks, where every activity contributes to growth of the corporate being (or becoming). Every action or reaction in the whole body, human or corporate, is a means of learning to perform more effectively next time – a concept often described as the 'learning organisation'. At all levels Rank–Xerox set up employee groups to seek business improvement, especially in quality but going beyond quality circles.

Many of the companies in the Ashridge data base work on this principle of continuous improvement (*kaizen* as the Japanese call it), where it is recognised that the people doing the actual job have vast resources of talent and understanding which it is foolish to leave untapped. The heritage of Taylorism was that it segregated thinkers from doers instead of recognising that the capacity to have ideas resided in every part of an enterprise.

Massey–Ferguson responded to a severe business slump in

[84]

the early to mid 1980s in farm machinery worldwide by the risk of open communication, conveying the sense of 'we're all in this together'. An early step management took was to hold a series of presentations to all workers in workshops, where the serious trade position was put on the table. Half the labour force was trained to be able to switch between machining and assembly. These steps were fundamental to getting the company on course by 1987. The workshops continued then as a means of combating complacency.

Thistle Hotels in the mid-1980s needed to ensure that all staff saw the customer in a new light. A key contribution was made by the monthly workshops for all staff. Full and part-time staff received social skills training run by the Scandinavian Service School. At all the various events employee suggestions were seriously mobilised. Suggestion schemes need to be handled properly, but they can be a highly motivational activity, so long as they are seen to be taken seriously and people are encouraged to offer the smallest suggestions as well as the major ones.

Quality and improvement circles

The French hypermarket Continent considered that quality was its key change issue. It introduced quality circles in a big way, but only after proper training and preparation. Daniel Maitre was appointed quality circle director after a training programme with the French Quality Circle Association, which under George Archier, head of a food-processing company, successfully transplanted these circles from their Japanese homeland. Their success was due to the participation of everyone, rather than a copycat following of Japanese collective cultural norms. Participation within well-specified and practical limits became a way of life in a French individualistic culture. It encouraged a move away from merely 'top down' management systems and changed the company's cultural mentality.

Maitre made a significant point when he said 'our training system teaches young people to participate in the learning process'. He is here defining the 'learning organisation' mentioned above. A successful organisation is a learning organisation, one where the whole organisation and all those who comprise it are on a continual voyage of discovery, living in expectation of new insights and finding them in each day's work. Learning is about change, because when you have learnt something, *you* have changed, as we saw in our first chapter, and you will in turn change something or somebody in your environment.

As in the Japanese companies visited by these French companies, *kaizen* became a way of life, where all employees were on the look out *all the time* for all the things they could improve, including the little things which in their own right or in total could make a big difference. This approach implies that no one is powerless. Everyone has some power to change something and should exercise it. Quality circles should not be viewed as an immutable system following a precise pattern. They need to be properly organised, but essentially they inspire a perspective whereby everyone is committed to a restless search for better ways of doing things – of serving the customer. Maitre saw them as making people more interested in their work, improving the company spirit and making it work better.

Continent's 7000 employees all took part in quality circles throughout the 1980s, beginning with a video programme, followed by meetings and training till, by the second half of the 1980s there were 100 quality circles in twenty-eight stores plus a top management quality circle. This vast programme was a proactive approach taken because it would enhance success. It was not put through in face of crisis, but when there was time to introduce the method carefully and fit it into the existing structure. UFB-Locabail, the French credit and leasing firm, an unusual business for quality circles, nevertheless introduced them, spending two years over the preparation.

Motorola holds seminars on the formulation of strategy and to help managers to understand the nature of the threat from the Asian Pacific Region. Jacobs–Suchard organised everyone in changes during the 1980s by publicising 'corporate themes', establishing 'rallying points', and 'selectively invoking martial law' to 'deal swiftly with crucial issues'. Ken Olsen worked to permeate Digital Equipment (DEC) with a sense of challenge, so that ultimate changes should be owned throughout the company, as flowing out of shared upheavals. The General Electric

Company has been using its Crotonville training centre to nurture a new breed of managers who will encourage initiative and ensure that its results are successful. Jack Welch, the CEO, says 'You want to open up the place so that people can flower and grow, expand, hit the home run. When you are tight bound, controlled, checked, nitpicked, you kill it.'

Technology

Technology is naturally enough a significant part of the change scenario. It is used to cut people costs; to speed up manufacturing and assembly processes; to capture information that makes money out of money, by having it in the right place in order to hold it in the best currency of the moment; and to facilitate the meeting of customer needs, anywhere, at any time, in the form it is wanted and with the minimum of physical material and the maximum of accompanying service. Technological change has a knock-on effect, so that change in this field in response to need becomes the trigger of further change. It pervades the data base, even though it has fewer specific mentions than one would have expected.

Imagination

Many of the other types in Table 7.2 are implicit in those we have been reviewing. The instilling of an entrepreneurial approach is frequently part of both organisational and people-oriented changes. Rank–Xerox develops networks of workers on contract to the company; 3M encourages people to go off and innovate. In addition, people-related changes often lead to imaginative changes in working hours and practices. Blue Circle Industries, the cement-based UK conglomerate, has removed overtime from its vocabulary by an annual hours policy; people benefit from getting work done in the fewest hours consistent with quality and with enhanced productivity. (For details of this kind of change in a number of companies see Curson, 1986.)

Internationalisation

Internationalisation of business did not feature as much in our source material as we had expected. Perhaps this highlights a danger of insularity still to be overcome, for there is no doubt that the shrinkage of the world, and the opening up of the whole planet as a global market, must cause companies who hitherto had confined their gaze to their own countries to see it as imperative to look beyond the confines of one country. This is already proving true even in companies of small or medium size, and, as we write, the changes in Eastern Europe are being seen as possible business opportunities.

Certainly, the change in transforming a domestic organisation to one with an international perspective requires the development of a different approach on the part of managers and all employees. Many of them may need to become physically mobile, but all need to become mentally mobile, as we saw in earlier chapters.

Summary

This chapter, then, has put some flesh on our theme. By using the Ashridge Change Data Base, we have seen examples of reactive change initiated to meet crisis and proactive change established to seize opportunities. We have seen the power of the chief executive to influence change, yet without reducing everyone's power to contribute something, however small, to successful change. We have considered how organisational structure can enhance personal opportunities, and above all how really effective change has to engage the hearts and minds of people. The reasons for change have to be clear, but people have to be helped emotionally to buy into it.

Chapter 8

CHANGES IN BRITISH BUSINESS AT THE START OF THE 1990s

In the course of recent research, Ashridge Management Research Group (AMRG) has had the opportunity to visit a number of British organisations, large and small, public and private sector. The original purpose was to learn how they were developing their managers, but in order to understand this major concern, it was inevitable that we would discuss the wider issues of developing the whole organisation and all the people in it, not only the managers. Very soon, in most of the companies, we were discussing change.

The results of this research for the UK Training Agency is published by AMRG under the title *People Development and Improved Business Performance*, (Wille, 1990). We have selected a few of the companies visited in order to illustrate a positive attitude to change in improving business performance. The organisations represent a variety of industries and business activities of various sizes. Our purpose will be the simple one of giving an up-to-date picture of some of the positive and exciting changes which are taking place, while recognising the problems they must initially have created.

Turning a company into a team

We visited IBC Vehicles in Luton which had introduced a new culture with amazing success. It had been riddled with industrial disputes and some three or four years ago had made record losses. The first step in the culture change was to negotiate a new contract with the trade unions on the site. The unions could hardly dispute the fact that if something positive were not done, there would soon be no company and no jobs for their members. Against this background they agreed, not without some heart-searching at first, that they would work with the management on a co-operative basis; the assumption that confrontation was the norm had to go.

The company promised openness and trust to provide an environment which would be conducive to co-operation. As an earnest of sincerity, common terms and conditions of working were introduced. Everyone had to use the same car park on a basis of 'first come, first served'. Even the chairman would have no special place. Everyone would use the same food-vending machines and the same microwave ovens to heat snacks. There would be no clocking in and all staff would have sick pay. Why should it be supposed that one part of the workforce was to be trusted more than another?

These steps might be thought of as symbolic or representative of a move to a soft human relations policy. But they gave a very clear signal that all the workforce were now to be regarded as belonging to one team, and that 'us and them' was a thing of the past.

The basic framework of the contract and of the agreement flowing from it were kept simple. They did not attempt to cover every detail as you might in a legal system or a rule book. It was a matter of establishing a spirit rather than a rigid code. The personnel director also said that it was seen only as a framework. Utopia would not arrive overnight or even ever. It was a matter of travelling hopefully rather than arriving. The journey mattered too, and with the rate of change in the industry the journey would never end. That is why it was so important to establish the right spirit and maintain it. All this was said with passion and obvious sincerity by a well-seasoned manager, who said he had never been so excited as he was by what was then happening in the company.

Another change introduced was organisational. Yet again it was a matter of enhancing attitudes and job interest, a matter of treating all the employees as having an intelligent contribution to make: 130 teams were set up as the structure for carrying out *all* the tasks of the company, team leaders were appointed and there were changes in the supervisory/foreman structure. Much more autonomy was left with the shop floor, it being recognised that the workers there were better informed about the detail of the job than anyone else.

All the employees, nearly 2000 of them, were given appraisal discussions, as of right, to discuss the job, their feelings about it and their progress and aspirations. To make this practical, the supervisory staff and anyone with people reporting to him or her received training in counselling and how to run appraisals. The average size of teams was ten to twelve, though office staff tended to be part of rather larger teams. There were regular team meetings to forward ideas about raising efficiency, and a productivity scheme which got everybody focusing on continuous improvement.

There was a suggestion scheme which actually worked, with both major awards for significant proposals and small discretionary sums of money for the smaller changes proposed.

It all sounded too good to be true, the kind of thing you read about in books about the Japanese approach, and which makes you say: 'Yes, but that's a different culture'. But the proof of the pudding is in the eating. In the first year after the changes the company moved into profit which has been maintained. There has not been a single hour lost in industrial action in the period. People are responding to being treated as people.

The company illustrates the fact that the key to successful change, even in times of dire trouble, is to be guided by empathy and to manage the situation with a full awareness of what it feels like to be the other people for whom you have responsibility. It's what consultant Roger Harrison calls 'love in the workplace', and it works.

Flexibility: quality: teamwork

Shortly after the above experience Edgar visited Nissan Motors (UK) (NMUK) in Sunderland and saw for himself the reality of the story told by Peter Wickens, director of personnel, in his

[91]

book *The Road to Nissan.* There are many similarities between the two stories, as Edgar here tells it:

My visit took place mainly in a large open-plan office where some 120 people worked with an opportunity to communicate or not, as they pleased. I was pleasantly surprised that my discussions felt as uninterrupted as if I had been in a private room. The staff apparently like it, because they feel they know what's going on. They are not shut out. Peter Wickens had his corner in the open office and, like most of his staff, wore the company blue jacket, trousers and shirt. It's voluntary, but it reduces status divisions (and saves money, as the company provides the clothing). The aim of this and other common terms and conditions is to remove all barriers. Like IBC Vehicles, there are none of the normal distinctions between classes of employee, even in things like sick pay, pensions and hospital treatment provision.

The company had a strong philosophy based on the three pillars of flexibility, quality and teamwork. Everyone thought of himself or herself as providing service to the next in line, who was the internal customer. The Japanese approaches had been modified to British taste, but the concept of *kaizen* predominated – the idea of continuous improvement (i.e. change) of everything by everybody.

The idea was to get the process right, with communications and relationships soundly founded, and the outcome was bound to be good. This differs from the results orientation, which focuses on the achievement and the outcome and is unconcerned about how you get there.

Everywhere, in the factory and in the offices, the day starts with a team meeting at 8.00 am. It lasts from five to fifteen minutes. Anything can be raised. Longer issues will be deferred to a later meeting of those concerned, but all know what is going on and all can contribute. An incidental effect is on timekeeping: peer pressure is enough to keep people from being late for the meeting.

Every team has its own area, with the leader's desk, a meeting space, microwave oven and similar facilities, and information display boards. Again, everyone is part of the appraisal process. A distance learning centre is available 24 hours a day, seven days a week, to everyone.

Line managers carry responsibility for people and resources and do not delegate it to specialists. Everyone has a say in strategy, constantly being invited to ask why they and the company are there, and what direction they want to take.

There are no job descriptions at all, because they are restrictive and impede the required flexibility. The Nissan approach also makes it difficult to single out a manager as someone separate, because in a sense every employee is a manager and decisions are made at the lowest level. But if managers must be defined separately, they are, as Doug Lorraine put it, those 'who manage the people so that the people can manage the task'. The aim of managing people is to bring out their energies and develop their skills.

Management redefined
The picture of a changed way of doing business continues with the story of Rothmans International, which I visited in Darlington the day after Nissan, and here there was no question of Japanese influence. Colin O'Neill helped an understanding of the principles by which Rothmans had operated in establishing two factories in north-east England.

Organisations were there to grow people. Say a group of people decided to do something – to go to the moon perhaps, or build cars – but they couldn't do it all themselves, and they needed people. Organisation was the way in which the people were grown to enable the vision or the idea to be fulfilled. Growing people, giving them accountability and responsibility, was the key activity of organisations and managers had this as their prime role.

The manager's job in Rothmans was to bring into full play the learning ability of the employees: to help the whole person – intellect, feeling and action – to contribute. The workers were all organised in teams, at every level. All shared concern with quality and improvement, with how to control waste and its cost. The job of team leaders was to make the teams self-managing. The managerial role was facilitative, its main activities being to counsel, to coach and to help people to learn. Managers did not solve problems for their teams, but enabled them to solve them for themselves, so that they would own the solutions and knowledge to handle the next problem.

Listening was a fundamental skill of managers in the Rothmans context, and the sharing of information, not the monopolising of it. The emphasis in all this learning was making the group more effective and not just the individual.

Colin O'Neill said that the teamworking approach was not an easy ride. It was in fact the most difficult way to manage, but the most satisfying, and it did lead to good bottom-line results. Readers are invited to take from these three stories of teamwork and changed business approaches whatever they can, and apply the principles to their own situations as far as they can.

It is not a matter of altruism, but of sound business sense, to liberate and utilise the full potential of people with bottom-line benefit.

A total quality management company

We visited McKechnie Extruded Products Ltd in the British Midlands, employing some 700 or 800 people, of whom 500 formed the shop-floor workforce. This workforce consisted largely of long-servers, 50 per cent having been with the company over twenty years, and, of this 50 per cent, 30 per cent having been with the company over thirty years. One might think this was not a promising kind of age distribution for change, but we have to get rid of the idea that you can't teach an old dog new tricks. Edgar is in the older age category and has learned more in the last five years working closely with Ashridge than he learned in the previous ten.

McKechnie's took a decision at board level to introduce total quality management (TQM). Since then everything has been affected by TQM, training and development particularly becoming of central significance.

First, the directors attended a top seminar and devised an excellent programme for the company. They issued a mission statement that 'operating performance will be continuously improved by the combined efforts and involvement of everybody in the business'. It went on to say how the continuous improvement was to be brought about by the process of measurement, communication and learning. Side by side with the training of all employees in TQM, organisational structure changes were undertaken so that every employee could become effective and flexible in job performance.

Training in TQM was first given to the thirty most senior managers – one week spread over a period of three months. This was to be continued at a later stage.

Simultaneously with the senior training, seven or eight middle managers and supervisors received training in the art of facilitating the learning of others. They received ten days' training and were then launched into facilitating the learning of the next seventy managers down the line. The training of these seventy managers began with a one-day workshop on a whole range of TQM-ish issues, after which the middle managers and supervisors moved into action teams to deal with specific cross-functional projects, both as a method of fixing their learning and in order to carry out needed activities. Smaller development teams were also introduced to work on specific improvement projects. Throughout, the facilitators would assist the development of the seventy, augmented by specific skills training from other sources as required.

The cascading of TQM throughout the whole management and supervisory structure then began to change perceptions about all the activities of the company. Everybody was going to be brought in, so styles of management had to be changed, and where previously there had been autocratic types of management, this approach just had to be modified, otherwise the outcomes required of managers would not be forthcoming. These objectives required the participation of everybody, down to an understanding at shop-floor level of statistical process control. There was some reduction in the numbers of staff on a voluntary basis, which was not the cause of any undue unrest. All managers and supervisory staff were being trained in appraisal techniques, so that all staff could have the benefit of constructive appraisal. A second batch of facilitators was being developed, some of them from the shop floor.

This company is now in the second year of all this change activity, but the progress achieved so far augurs well for its future. It is, like our other companies in this chapter, so far moving in the direction of becoming a learning organisation, i.e. an organisation where everything that is done is used as a means of doing it better and thereby securing competitive edge.

When quality forces growth

The next story is about a small engineering components firm in Luton employing sixty people: Stanbridge Precision Turned Parts Ltd.

As soon as you walk into the company, you get a feeling that it is a family. Everybody works with everybody else, and there is a good deal of flexible skill encouragement. However, the change problem in this company relates to growth. A population of sixty is not too many for a family spirit, but if it increases in order to accept the amount of work that is available, then this family spirit could well become eroded, and the managing director, Bob Knox, would have to delegate some of the tasks he enjoys handling personally.

In addition, one of the large companies that this small organisation supplies has proposed that it should join its super quality scheme. To gain this seal of approval would certainly be quite a prize, and would ensure the continuance of business with the larger company. However, it would require the employment of a statistical process controller and a trainer, the provision of proper accommodation for training, the establishment of quality circles as well as highly sophisticated procedures to ensure that quality was built into all products first time.

Now here is a case of the dilemma 'to change or not to change'. If the company expands to meet the extra cost of going down this high quality avenue (and the quality is already above average in the company), then the family spirit may be lost and even some of the high productivity may consequently be reduced. There may also be changes in the quality of life enjoyed by the managing director himself, who had to work round the clock in the earlier days but now can delegate much more activity, and in the quality of life of the employees, who have a highly committed but relaxed environment.

Part of this growth problem also relates to getting enough

high quality staff in an area where, as soon as you train somebody, there are other organisations that don't go in for training
ready to auction for your trained staff. Well, the decision has
been made to go ahead with the high quality standard, which
means that everybody in the company will receive special TQM
training, and everybody will be seeking constantly to improve
everything that is done – a principle which is already broadly
being followed.

However, the company will never be the same again. The
managing director felt that all his staff knew that he thought
they were important to the success of the company and that this
mood already permeated it. He feared this might be more
difficult if it grew too much though a year later its spirit is being
maintained.

This is an interesting story of change and potential change
that is probably characteristic of a number of small, successful
companies with fairly safe markets.

'Everything is everybody's business'

We visited a company making specialised automobiles. A considered decision was made to move away from the traditional
autocratic method of controlling the shop floor, with much
swearing and shouting. It was recognised, with strong encouragement from the personnel manager, that talent at the shop
floor needed to be harnessed and the workers' commitment
established. Appraisal schemes and team briefing became a
regular feature, even though some managers could not regard
them as necessary. At the management level regular meetings
held every Friday now discussed what the company as a whole
was doing, and not just what particular managers were concerned with.

This, in turn, meant that when the management team met
the shop-floor committees, all the line managers were concerned with all the functions, instead of leaving it to non-line
functional people like personnel to deal with certain issues.

We were being told that the whole workforce was being
encouraged to take responsibility for quality – electricians were
diagnosing their own faults, and when a workman noticed that

something was wrong, he took action himself rather than letting it go through for an inspector to ring it round. We smiled to ourselves, thinking that this was another good story. However, just at that moment one of the workmen came in to report that he had just gone through the conference room and had noticed a leak over the stage. He said it was none of his business, actually, but he thought he ought to report it so that maintenance could deal with it.

We're quite sure this was not a little drama enacted for our benefit, but it certainly illustrated the idea that everything was everybody's business. The idea of quality being everybody's responsibility was encouraging the company to move from piecework into measured daywork. On piecework the only interest seemed to be getting the stuff, good, bad or indifferent, on to the next stage, so that the appropriate wages could be earned. A bonus scheme based on profit, cashflow and stock levels was being introduced and was already in operation for the management. One of the interesting things that had happened since introducing the scheme was that the managers them-selves, as part of their managerial functions, determined what money was available. If one of them failed to deliver the goods, he would be reducing the bonus for his/her colleagues. Thus, peer pressure was brought to bear on improved performance. There are all kinds of ways in which change is implemented.

Of other companies we visited, at least half a dozen had some form or other of change workshops, where new attitudes or an understanding of the company mission was cascaded down throughout the whole organisation on a basis which gave every-body a chance to have his/her say about what was going on.

Customer service in the public sector

We visited some local authorities in the UK. Since they have been required to act as agents for the community in order to ensure that the services are available rather than necessarily providing them themselves, a great change has been brought about. It has meant that local authorities are setting out to be enablers rather than just providers, with a concern with what the customer wants rather than what professional people think customers ought to want, with a community-building vision rather than a dependency-creating approach. In addition, some of them see their role as helping their area to function as if it were a business.

All this has meant a fundamental change in the world of the local authorities, with a need to move to a customer-driven approach instead of a bureaucratic committee and provision approach. New management skills are required, such as evaluation, quality, cost-benefit analysis, customer monitoring, performance evaluation and freedom to try things which previously were unthinkable. This is a total culture change. Some of the older staff, who have done worthy work, have been happy to retire rather than adapt to the new style. One council has set up 700 cost centres as a means of establishing responsibility and accountability. This could be quite alarming for people who have had an easy routine ride hitherto. There are management audits being established to see how far various indicators are being met.

On the positive side, there is no doubt that talent is being liberated by the increased responsibility being given. Organisations where it is possible to do things without waiting for a ruling all the time are being created. There is scope to act, to risk and even to fail sometimes. Constraints from the centre are being reduced, which gives an opportunity for people to develop.

Nottinghamshire county council has introduced some interesting approaches in its educational institutions. Schools and colleges all over the county were invited to select, by a vote of all the teaching staff, someone to be trained as a consultant to the school. The training consisted of a month's input on how to be a consultant and a counsellor, to listen and to help the process of change. This was followed by three months' full-time work on change issues in the school, alongside the teachers, with all their problems, and then one day a week for another eight months, after which the role became a permanent one.

This has proved a very successful intervention over a period of four years and certainly has helped both the effectiveness and the efficiency, as well as the morale, of the teaching staff. Such an approach could well be thought about in private business and industry.

Ind Coope brews beer with a difference

We finish this chapter with one of the most remarkable stories that we have met. It is a story of how, over a period of five years, the Ind Coope Brewery in Burton-on-Trent transformed its whole working arrangements. The story is told by ex-managing director David Cox in his book *By GABB and by GIBB* (Greenfield Assessment Burton Brewery and Greenfield Implementation Burton Brewery).

The brewing industry was facing difficulty as a result of the growing market share of lager, which was eroding the normal beer market. A small working party had already started to look for practical ways of providing more efficient and satisfying work by combining various work functions within the company. It showed up many weaknesses and created a realisation that the traditional approach would not do for the future. This led to the establishment of a group of managers to engage in 'green field' thinking – a comprehensive reappraisal of every facet of the business without constraint. They could even decide whether the brewery should stay in Burton-on-Trent, and in the initial thinking even money was not to be a constraint. The traditional world of these managers was turned on its head, with the idea of unlocking creativity, gaining commitment, and allowing the development of ideas that could be the property of groups of individuals. The study was then expanded, and four different groups got to work on marketing, operations, personnel, payments and overall management.

The MD kept out of the actual discussions, making his contribution as a listener when required, to protect the experimental approach from higher echelons in the corporate group until something was ready.

Eventually the groups reported, suggesting revolutionary changes to the processing, the packaging, and the by-product handling, and proposing a new single warehouse for all packed goods. Before GABB (assessment) could move to GIBB (implementation), a period for all employees to express their views was going to be allowed. This was particularly critical, as the number of employees was going to be reduced considerably over the next five years, but without the need for enforced redundancies.

[100]

A meeting was held with the whole of the workforce, in which questions were answered honestly and the answers published, so that all could have them as a small brochure. Throughout the time scale of the four or five years, there were regular presentations and bulletins to keep everybody aware that the whole issue was a matter of working together for their future. Every detail was shared with the whole staff, and a lot of excitement was generated. David Cox was not frightened in the slightest of banging the drum and saying such things as 'Leaders won't go far wrong if they treat people in the same way that they expect to be treated themselves'. He made clear that the keys for the success of the company lay in frankness, readiness to change, planning, mutual pressure, trust, flexibility, example and courage.

In terms of organisation to meet the changes the basic building block would be working teams. For each working team the following were identified: the overall task, the half dozen or so key tasks, the decisions the team would be required to take for the tasks to be carried out effectively, and those for which they would need to consult others. For each key task there would be a review mechanism by which the team would be able to judge its own performance. These teams would be left to get on with their own tasks. All the artificial demarcations between colleagues would be swept away.

Well, it actually happened, and Figure 8.1 (reproduced by permission of David Cox and Ind Coope) illustrates the organisation structure diagram at Spring 1988. It will be seen that everybody was a member of a team which, in turn, linked in with another team, and each team leader was a member of the next team up, all at last linking up with the executive. It looks very different from the normal organisation chart.

The selection of the team leaders was an adventurous activity. Everybody, other than the managing director, had to apply for his/her own job under the new title of team leader of this function or that function, although for outside purposes some could keep their title, like the chief brewer. Fourteen role skills were identified for the team leaders, and a common language was used to describe each one of them, together with some examples. The role skills identified were:

Achiever	Motivator
Communicator	Persuader
Conciliator	Planner
Deployer	Quality maintainer
Developer	Representative
Improver	Resource provider
Missionary	Team worker

A booklet described what each of these words meant. Selection of the team leaders was made from some 320 people who put in for the 160 jobs. All had the opportunity to pass through an assessment centre, which was also a development centre. Every effort was made to enable it to be a pleasant experience, in that nobody was going to lose, though some were going to gain. It was called a team development programme rather than a selection effort. Those who did not get the team-leader jobs had their efforts noted for further purposes, and many of them did in fact later get team-leader jobs.

The whole activity produced a basic culture change, where after initial confrontations the place became a large set of teams where honesty, openness and trust, together with a determination to share with every employee, actually became reality. It was recognised that there was no other way for the business to survive and grow.

For those whose services would not be required, a new work department was established to assist them to set up in small businesses. In the event, the number of people requiring this help was so small that the approach was not followed through.

Common terms and conditions and harmonious remuneration plans were implemented. These were the last to be accepted, and a fairly tough set of negotiations had to take place before they were agreed.

The story sounds too good to be true, and of course with change of management at the top modifications will inevitably happen. Moreover, one cannot assume that because an organisation has been transformed, it will necessarily be able to stand up to the external forces that will always bear down upon everybody. However, at the time that David Cox wrote his book, he made it clear that the greenfield implementation of Burton Brewery was never a social experiment, it was a capital

[102]

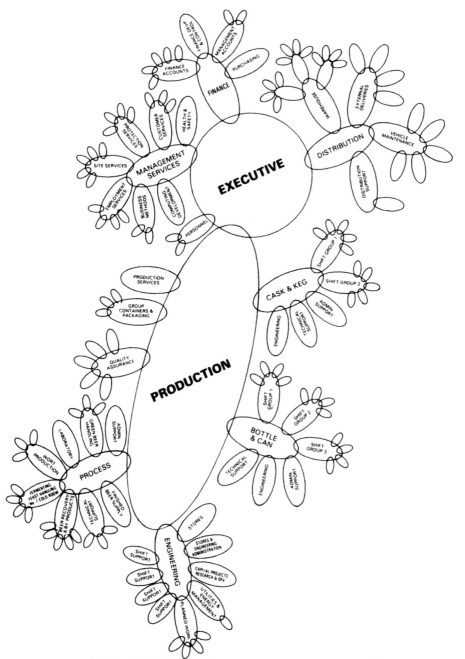

FIG. 8.1 The full ICBB organisation structure as at Spring 1988

investment programme whose objective was primarily cost-saving and bottom line. In order to achieve these practical business objectives, it was essential to unify the aspirations of the people, so that competitive advantage could be gained. The central theme was a people strategy based on team working applied to all facets of the business.

Financial objectives were achieved. The last statement in the book is that this achievement was not the end: 'One of the cornerstones of the project was acceptance of change and continuing change is the only certainty for the future'.

There is a postscript in the book from Price Waterhouse, the accountant/consultancy firm. The key paragraph in it is as follows:

Not having known the climate of industrial relations in ICBB (Ind Coope Burton Brewery) at the time GIBB started, we cannot verify the assertion that the climate has been transformed or that its beneficial impact on willingness and commitment has been remarkable. We certainly can say, however, that we found a company of people who displayed a spirit of mutual trust, co-operation and team working which was refreshing, greatly encouraging and well worth fostering. The company has basic facilities essential to low cost, high volume, high variety production, but of equal importance it has people who are all pulling in the same direction, aiming to exploit the opportunities now open to them.

Summary

This chapter has aimed to give the flavour of some change-welcoming companies visited in the course of the recent Ashridge research, which has enabled us to go into companies and see what successful change is like on the ground floor. For Edgar, who undertook most of the visits, it was certainly an experience which helped to allay the cynicism that one sometimes feels when reading the story of success. Here were companies actually doing excellent things in pursuance of positive change. As the object of this book is to aid the development of a change mindset which is oriented towards the future rather than rooted in the past, it was felt important by the authors to include material that was optimistic and encouraging while still being realistic. If the companies that we have been talking about can do such things, can't your company similarly achieve positive and beneficial change? We make no apologies for being slightly evangelical on the matter. We pose you a question as a challenge: what changes in your organisation would you like to be boasting about in two years' time?

Note to reader as co-author
Add here or in your exercise book the changes you would like your organisation to be able to boast about in two years' time.

_____

_____

_____

_____

_____

_____

_____

_____

_____

_____

_____

_____

_____

[105]

Chapter 9

MORE POWER THAN YOU THINK YOU HAVE

Throughout this book we have been trying to envisage our audience as consisting of all the people in an enterprise. We have been seeking to address not only the board and the senior management, but also the middle and junior management, the supervisors and the people on the shop floor. All are necessary to the success of the company, all have a role to play in the essential change activities which lie at the heart of success.

Nevertheless, the triggers for change, to which we referred in Chapter 7, did tend to be considering changes introduced from the top. However, there was recognition that top pressure without response further down the line would not achieve its objectives.

Chapter 8, by giving more detailed specific examples out of our own experience, did give illustrations of power to influence change at all levels in an organisation. We had influence being shared, ideas cascading all the way down to everybody. We had teamwork: we saw examples of the divide between management and workforce being eroded. However, the initiative tended to come from the top, and indeed this is a normal source of leadership.

We have tried throughout this book, however, to avoid the implication that only the top can change anything. We observe that many books on change tend to concentrate on the board as the strategists and policy-makers within a company. Some books also deal with the implementing of change where less senior people are obviously required to carry out plans that have been developed higher up the pyramid. They may or may not have helped in the working out of the plans.

Thus it is possible that readers at a less senior level may feel that this book is all very well, but how does it help them carry out their own functions in relation to change? You may be one of these and feel a certain sense of powerlessness. You may feel the victim of change, rather than the constructive initiator of it for the good of the company and for your own benefit.

The message of this chapter is that you have more power than you think you have. Even if, as Tables 7.1 and 7.2 indicate, chief executive officers and people at that level dump change initiatives at your feet (or on your head), they still depend upon you for success in making their vision into reality.

Indeed, the first few chapters of this book were intended to encourage everybody to develop a change mindset and a future mindset that looked at the present from the perspective of possible futures. We wanted everybody at all levels in an enterprise to feel comfortable with, and even welcome, change.

So how can non-policy-making managers and people positively affect the course of change?

If the change which is introduced invites participation, there is no difficulty, unless the difficulty be lack of the skills to implement what is being proposed. But IBC Vehicles, McKechnie's Extruded Products and Stanbridge Precision Turned Parts mentioned in the previous chapter obviously did invite all staff to participate in the change programme, and made sure that they received the training and encouragement to play their part. The story of Ind Coope in Burton-on-Trent was an outstanding example of general participation and effective teamwork. Here change was proactive, there was no sense of crisis, but rather a determination to get ahead in the game before unwelcome changes invaded the territory. Likewise the exciting stories of Nissan and Rothmans.

However, change often descends upon you in a way that you can only react to, and a proactive stance is difficult.

Making your part work

Even then, the change mindset and the future mindset will help not only acceptance but a positive approach. You want your

[108]

company to succeed because it employs you and you want to continue in employment, so what is the use of grumbling about the unwelcome change? Surely the sensible way is to try to understand it, and make your bit work. However, if you feel that you are being treated just as a machine or automaton, or even as a moron, you do have a difficulty. However, the bosses can't be on your tail all the time, and surely there must be a way out of the situation.

Do you really believe that you have no influence? When you go to work in a change situation, will nothing you do make any difference?

You can start by remembering the words of Ben Thompson-McCausland, that significant corporate change cannot be achieved by one man alone and that the organisation exists in the hearts and minds of everybody working in it, not in its balance sheets, buildings or computers. Thus, Sir John Harvey-Jones could only have turned ICI around provided he had support from the people for whom he wanted work to be fun. Thistle Hotels had to create an environment in which people were actually so influenced by it that they started being effective in their customer relations.

Perhaps you feel that the management of your organisation has not the vision of some of these people we have been quoting. But think about it. You don't have to have a lot of power in order to improve the quality of the work that you, your peers and your subordinates perform. You don't have to wait for a Total Quality Management programme to descend from on high; you don't have to wait for the training department in order to start coaching, mentoring, guiding and encouraging your subordinates or even your peers.

Influence is something that resides within you if you choose to stir it up. You can develop your own management style, which will include being concerned to develop the people for whom you are responsible in their skills, their approach to quality and their general attitudes to the job and the company.

The good examples that we have given were of managers who positively and consciously empowered others. If you are not in the situation where empowerment is offered to you, then don't you have to seize it? Don't you have to recognise that in your own thinking and behaviour there is latent power waiting to emerge?

The empowered manager

Peter Block has written a book called *The Empowered Manager* of which the subtitle is 'Positive Political Skills at Work'. His theme is that middle managers are not powerless; they can change things for their own unit and through that have a wider influence on the company culture. Change does not only start at the top.

Peter Block's theme at times may sound a little unreal, but he suggests that all members of an organisation should regard their own units as if they were their own businesses, and so create an organisation of their own choosing. Even if it were their own business, there would still be outside constraints which they would have to wrestle with. A well-known management writer of a previous generation, Chester Barnard, used to say that top people can only really run things with the permission of those they think they control. It is the old story that you can take a horse to the water but you cannot make it drink. Peter Block suggests to us that each time we act as a living example of how we want the whole organisation to operate, this is a positive political act and it will influence others. Block inspires us to take hold of the belief that the most trustworthy source of authority comes from within a person, and that the task of supervision is to help people trust their instincts and take their own responsibility for success. Even if you have only one person reporting to you, you can take this approach with them, and if you have none, you are still an influencer of others, as we shall see shortly.

People like Jan Carlzon of SAS have understood these principles, and have empowered people by emphasising that every time they are face to face with a customer, they have power to make or break the company. He looked at the role of top management not as dictation but support, and he actually inverted the hierarchical triangle and put the broad base at the top, with himself as chief executive at the base of the upturned triangle. Top management is there to help the rest perform.

However, that is an ideal and it may not exist in your company. But perhaps your company has decentralised – many do these days – which means driving decision down. If decision comes down, then seize the opportunity and don't be

[110]

frightened of the opportunity to decide, whatever the risks, to take courses of action without consulting but instead following your own instincts.

Donald Kirkpatrick, in his book *How to Manage Change Effectively*, addresses the need to help managers recognise the extent to which they have power to influence change, and that it isn't only the chief executive officer who can do this. He says that three roles apply to all managers: to implement changes decided by higher management; to pass up their own ideas for change or those of their subordinates to higher management; and to get on with initiating changes without such referral. Two out of the three are possible activities for managers at every level. The second has to be handled with sensitivity and awareness of the danger, but not on that account to be disregarded.

Trusting people

Donald Cantor and Philip Mervis, in their book *The Cynical Americans*, speak of the cynical 1980s. What they are saying doesn't apply only to Americans. The subtitle is 'Living and Working in an Age of Discontent and Disillusion'. It is this spirit that will prevent us from doing our part in the change activity but, as Peter Block says, even though there are dangers out in the world and there are times when it may look like a jungle, there is a substantial number of people ready to show trust and produce results. It all rather reminds one of us of what his step-grandmother told him when he was quite young: 'Edgar, you must look for the good in people'. Unfortunately we prefer to look for the bad. The Quakers have a belief that God is in every person; if you can't find God, at least you might find good in the most surprising places.

Kouzes and Posner, in their book *The Leadership Challenge*, speak of the high truster who says, 'I will trust this person until I have clear evidence that he or she cannot be trusted'. The low truster says, 'I will not trust this person until there is clear evidence that he or she can be trusted'. There is all the difference in the world between these two approaches.

All this is homespun morality, common sense, good manners, call it what you will. However, there is the kind of approach that assumes that people can and will, if you believe in them, be fundamental to the success of the change programme of an organisation. Peter Block uses the word 'power' in the non-coercive, positive sense, and declares that whether for a unit, the whole organisation, or a programming section bedded in the basement of an administrative service division, you yourself have power. To feel empowered means that we feel our survival is in our own hands; we don't blame others or speak all the time of those vague entities called 'they'.

Constructive disobedience

Our original definition of management began with the phrase risking yourself and entrusting and empowering people, encouraging them to act decisively on their own. There is danger in this course, for it is always possible that they may let you down. When he was at British Coal, Edgar used to speak every month to the junior management course in Newcastle-upon-Tyne and recommended to them that they learned the art of constructive disobedience. The phrase got round and he was once called to account by an area director, who had heard that Edgar Wille had been telling the staff not to do as they were told. That was not exactly his purpose, but he certainly was recommending that too much compliance, immediately doing as you're told, even when you can see a better way, is ultimately not to the benefit of the individual or the organisation.

Russell L. Akoff of Wharton Business School writes: 'If I could add only one subject to business school curricula, it would be that of how to beat the system. Beating the system means making a well designed system work poorly or a poorly designed system work well'. Sharon Kneeland writes on breaking the rules: 'It's easier to ask forgiveness than permission . . .' (what is the worse thing that can happen if I do?). Harvey Hornstein (1986) writes about 'managerial courage' as a way of revitalising your company without sacrificing your job.

Love in the workplace

Having an influence on change in your organisation does not mean waiting for somebody to give you some formal authority.

[112]

You can inspire people around you. You can coach, guide and encourage even if no one has told you to; and certainly you don't have to wait for a board decision to carry out the message in the song by Vivian Ellis: 'Spread a little happiness as you go by'. A smile will go a long way if it is genuine, and people soon know whether it is or not.

The consultant Roger Harrison writes a very small book called *Organisation Culture and Quality of Service*. It's the subtitle that impresses one: 'A strategy for releasing love in the workplace'. He uses the word 'love' in the sense of the Greek word *agape*, which is a love that serves and cares, rather than seeks its own gratification. The word *eros* was used by the Greeks for the latter. Roger Harrison knew that he was putting his consultancy, and therefore his power to earn money, on the line when he started talking about love. His vision, as he conceived it at the outset, was that he wanted to balance the powers of intellect and of the human will in organisations with the powers of intuition and of love. Imagine his pleasure in his postbag, with letters such as the one from someone who had felt alone in thinking that it was possible to work with people in such a caring atmosphere that the bottom line became a by-product of that atmosphere.

The current literature on service, illustrated by books such as Albrecht and Zemke's *Service America*, suggests the idea of loving your customer. If you don't like the word 'love', consider the word 'empathy', where you aim for the attitude of mind in which you have some idea of what it feels like to be the other person and then act accordingly.

Whatever it is you make or provide in your organisation, it is a service to others; and even though it is intended to earn you some monetary reward, it will only do this if the service is satisfactory. Roger Harrison says, 'A lot of people want to give warmer service than they are permitted to'. In his experience people who give service, whether internally or to the public, are more often frustrated by the circumstances, systems and procedures under which they must operate, than they are by the people they serve. Surely there is something that everybody, at whatever level, can do to inspire positive change in the direction of these thoughts.

When Roger Harrison, in the course of his consultancy, talks to leaders and managers about balancing achievement with support in their organisations, he encounters far more wistful looks in the audience than there are antagonistic ones. So although we talk about competitive edge, and Harrison is not unmindful of the need for profit, he actually believes that a more nurturing and responsive attitude in our business lives will be best for the business. He acknowledges that a change of approach has risks. The relaxation of controls can permit sloppy performance as well as service from the heart, and it will only work if the process is managed from the heart – not just because it is good business, but because it feels right.

The support culture

Roger Harrison recognises that this approach is simple but also hard. It is hard because most organisation cultures don't support the development of the heart. It is simple because there are certain behaviours which, practised faithfully, will open the heart of the one who practises and will 'warm the hearts of those impacted'. Roger Harrison gives us the reply that he offers when business leaders ask him what he means in practice by love in the business. He suggests that they treat other people and the organisation in the following ways:

- Give credit for their ideas and build on their contributions.
- Listen to their concerns, hopes, fears, pain; be there for them when they need an empathetic ear.
- Treat their feelings as important.
- Be generous with your trust. Give them the benefit of the doubt.
- See them as valuable and unique in themselves, and not simply for their contribution to the task.
- Respond actively to others' needs and concerns; give help and assistance when it is not your job.
- Look for the good and the positive in others, and acknowledge it when you find it.
- Nurture their growth: teach, support, encourage, smooth the path.
- Take care of the organisation. Be responsive to and responsible for its needs as a living system.

[114]

We can all do something along these lines, though it does mean starting with ourselves, with a determination not to be embarrassed by such a soft approach being displayed in the hard place that the organisation often is.

Hunger for community

Roger Harrison is not alone. Marvin R. Weisbord (1987) had first-hand business experience of running the family printing business before moving on to management consulting via teaching. He says that we hunger for community in the work-place and are a great deal more productive when we find it. Some of the illustrations we gave in Chapter 8 support this thought. His book *Productive Workplaces* is an enlivening presentation of the various approaches to management expressed by people ranging from Taylor to Lewin, MacGregor, Trist and Emery, and later writers. Lewin's thinking gave birth to participative management: 'To understand the system you must seek to change it. Thus change is the essence of running a business'. The same theme pervades Weisbord's writing: 'The aim of management must be to discover what seeds of growth (change) are already present among workers and to nourish these seeds'. Work should not limit personal potential but develop it. 'Give workers a sense of significance which is productive and they will give to the business an awareness whose importance can not be overestimated.' When the whole workforce take charge of their own lives, instead of living in dependency, then the company will thrive.

This chapter is fairly philosophic, but it expresses practical realities, such as are manifest in teamwork of which we have already seen examples. The essence of Weisbord's guidelines for change lies in one of his statements: 'To make a whole life we can live with, each of us has to become expert at integrating what we have to contribute with what others have'. Phil has a good story out of his own experience to illustrate this.

Phil's story: the power of self-help

Some years ago I worked for British Transport Hotels (BTH), a satellite of British Rail (BR). In the process of privatisation

[115]

virtually all the staff at head office were made redundant. Some were offered jobs within the BR group; 150 managers were not. Many of them had worked for the hotel group for most of their lives; they were unfamiliar with the process of seeking another job. BR itself didn't believe it had much need for hotel management skills, so it wasn't expected that many staff would find alternative jobs within the group. The morale of the 150 people plummeted.

A few of us decided that we could do more to find ourselves jobs within the huge BR group. We organised our 150 managers into 'sales' teams. The salesmen were to go round every corner of the British Rail empire and try to sell the one product they knew well, i.e. themselves and their colleagues. Most of them had no sales experience at all. The notion of the cold call, of going to see managers from completely different disciplines, was daunting. We started with the people most inclined towards selling. They then influenced some of the more reluctant managers. Thus we rapidly established a large team of people spending a significant part of each week visiting British Rail branches and subsidiaries in the search for jobs for the 150.

We were very successful. Partly I think this was because most British Rail managers had never been approached in this way before. None of us knew anything about high-powered sales techniques, but the honesty of our approach and the openness of our discussion impressed a lot of people. The 150 soon started to reduce in number. We also got together regularly in groups to talk about how things were going and to maintain morale. News of jobs coming up was quickly passed to people most likely to get them. Our information system was second to none.

One minor piece of technology helped us. Often when we visited a general manager, he would ask us about the ages, qualifications, or locations of the managers within our 150. We got hold of a micro-computer when these devices were still fairly rare in business. With the permission of the 150 participants, we put their basic personnel details on a data base on the micro-computer. We were then able to draw from the data base lists of staff tailored to the needs of particular employing managers in the BR system.

This had two positive effects. It gave our own 'sales people' a great boost to think they were using what was then quite modern technology, and it also impressed a number of the managers they were visiting, who saw that we were well organised and were prepared to chase our objectives with all the available technology we could lay our hands on.

It was a difficult time for everyone, and of course morale didn't stay high all the time. But by the end of the period almost all the 150 had been offered jobs, and most maintained their self-confidence during a very difficult time. They had more power than they thought.

Choices for the manager

Rosemary Stewart (1982) invites managers to consider their work under three headings: the demands of the job, the constraints of the job and the choices. The demands are what you have to do, the constraints are the factors which tend to stop you from doing it and the choices are where you are free either to initiate work or decide how it is to be done. Everybody's aim must be to meet the demands and overcome the constraints as effectively as possible, so that they can get on with the real contribution that they are uniquely able to make by their own choices. It is the choices that people follow that create the entrepreneurial approach in business. Phil's team of 'self-sellers' were exercising choices in their entrepreneurial activity. Choices give one a sense of freedom which pervades the whole of the work. So this too is reflective of our theme that you have more power to change things than you think you have.

Rosemary Stewart also emphasises the power of networking. If one of the definitions of management is getting results through others, you don't even have to have staff working for you in order to be a manager. You can mobilise relationships and attract resources even though you have no formal authority over anybody. This is where networking comes in.

She portrays the idea of networking in a very simple diagram, from which Figure 9.1 is derived. Again, we invite you to participate in this chapter. You are in the middle of this diagram and the outer circles are the key contacts that you have built up – through them you can exercise your influence and get results. Either write in the book or take some photocopies of Figure 9.1 and fill in the initials of people through whom you get results. They are your network. They are your source of power. Leonard Sales, in 1966, defined the importance of the manager's network of contacts: 'The one enduring objective of the manager is the effort to build and maintain a predictable, reciprocating system of relationships'.

My Network

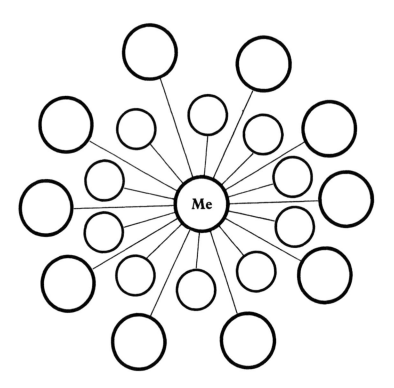

Insert the initials of people with whom you need contact to achieve your objectives. Use the inner ring of circles for people in your network within your organisation and the outer ring for those in your network outside.

FIG. 9.1   My network, based on the diagram by Rosemary Stewart (1982)
Choices

Rosemary Stewart asks a series of questions:

- Who is in my network? That is, whom do I know well enough to ask for information or favours?
- Who is not there whom it would be useful to have within it?
- How effective are each of those contacts for getting the information and support that I may need?
- What can be done to strengthen a relationship and/or develop a new one?
- Who might want to help in supporting a specific plan?
- What price may I have to pay for seeking help? Have I overdrawn the balance of goodwill?
- What kind of exchange does each member of the network value?
- What exchanges, trades, have I got to offer a particular contact?

Power and influence beyond formal authority

J.P. Kotter (1985) in a book with the above title contrasts the traditional organisational chart with the complex of networks through which modern leaders get their results. He very clearly indicates ways whereby people who have no formal authority to tell others what to do can nevertheless achieve their objectives. He has quite a bit to say therefore about managing your boss, which includes finding ways to learn about the boss's goals, pressures, strengths, weaknesses and working style, while being sensitive to one's own and doing one's best to match the two in an attempt to create a good working relationship. All too often we are irritated by those elements in the boss's style that we find unhelpful. However, we are not going to change them, so we might as well understand them and act accordingly, without becoming obsequious.

John Kotter talks about networks where managers need to identify all the relevant relationships that can help them; assess who may resist co-operation, and why and how strongly; and then develop good relationships which will overcome most kinds of resistance. It is no good, he says, thinking of the job simply in terms of the technical skill it requires or the management power it may have. All jobs have to be thought of in relational terms. It is important to ask a series of questions such as the following: What am I trying to achieve in my work? What are the key tasks this year, this month, this week, today? For each of these tasks, whose co-operation will be necessary and whose compliance will be necessary? One may then go ahead in the light of this awareness.

Kotter gives examples of managers whose jobs cannot proceed without this approach. For instance, a product manager of a large firm has revenue and income responsibility for some product line; he or she is absolutely dependent on the people who make the product, who advertise it, sell it, distribute it, and so forth. Perhaps there are thousands of these people, yet none reports to the product manager. They are located in different chains of command or even outside the product manager's firm, but it is his or her responsibility so to organise the network that the whole thing hangs together and produces success.

This chapter has aimed to encourage the manager who doubts his or her own power to see that it is there for the taking, even though it will require a lot of perseverance and development to ensure that it is exercised. We hope that readers will not be put off by the fact that we have, with people like Harrison and Weisbord, not shrunk from emphasising the inward emotional and almost spiritual requirements of effective management, particularly when it comes to managing change. We need the hard and the soft skills in correct balance to achieve success.

Note to reader as co-author
Add here or in your exercise books a story or two of where you realised or realise now that you had more power than you at first thought.

_____

_____

_____

_____

_____

Chapter 10

THE LITTLE THINGS THAT MAKE A BIG DIFFERENCE

In Chapter 9 we concentrated on the attitude which a manager who is not at the top of the organisation can employ to influence those for whom he or she is responsible and, indeed, peers and other parts of the organisation. We talked of teamwork and love and community, of networking, of choices, of management styles, of caring attitudes, of managing the boss and nurturing relationships. We saw that power does not simply rest in formal authority or organisational level, but in ideas and attitudes. Now we want to see how this power you didn't know you'd got is often exercised in the little things.

It's not only the big things that make a difference. It's the specific little actions that often mean so much. Broad attitudes alone will not create a warm workplace; there has to be a smile or an action which is an expression of love and care. In this chapter we shall be recognising that nothing is too minor, too unimportant to introduce positive change in the work environment. It may be as simple as everybody picking up rubbish whenever they see it. Where this has been done, a whole workplace has assumed a new appearance, and the new appearance has helped people's attitudes to the job, establishing a quality approach.

One of the organisations that we have visited in the project referred to in Chapter 8 issues tie-pins or brooches to its staff. On them is inscribed 'It matters to me'.

Little things in an overseas factory

Edgar did some work overseas for the International Labour

Office (ILO) and on one occasion ran a workshop on the little things that make a big difference. He challenged the managers at a chemical factory to come with him to the window and guaranteed to find some little things that anybody could do, and for which no authority was required, in order to improve conditions. The managers crowded around the window and Edgar immediately said, 'Yes, look, there is that hole there. I have been coming here for two months. It was there the first day I came, it is there now, covered by a rather rocky piece of concrete. Anyone could go and move that and put some proper covering on the hole. And, while you're about it, you could also ask why is the hole there anyway?'

Then they listened and from one of the machines opposite came a strange clonking sound. Edgar said, 'Why is it making that noise? I am not an engineer, but is it really supposed to?' 'Oh no,' said one, 'he simply hasn't oiled it today.' So, with a mixture of humour and challenge, Edgar wanted to know how such things could be allowed to go on. He could only hope that some ears took the point before the machine ground to a halt.

Phil has a story to tell in this regard.

Phil's story of a human face

This is a story about my wife Jane and me as customers. Jane was expecting our second child and had been admitted to hospital somewhat early because of concern for the baby. The hospital was on the outskirts of London, a huge grey concrete anonymous building – grey outside and grey inside. On first impression it was an unwelcoming place.

We found the ward, my wife was shown to her bed and we waited for the doctor. Up to then no one had spoken to us, except to give directions or ask for information to log us into the system. We felt like small particles in a huge machine. We had not been able to express our personal worries about mother and child.

A nurse put her head round the curtain and said, 'The Doctor's coming, he'll be with you in a moment'. He arrived and immediately changed everything for us by his unexpected action. Instead of saying, 'Hello, I'm Doctor Smith', he came round the bed, shook Jane's hand, shook my hand and said, 'Hello, I'm John Smith'. No mention of Doctor or anything else like that. He got to work examining Jane and talking all the time not just about the medical aspect of what he was doing, but also about the concerns she and I felt. He obviously could see that we were quite tense.

This man made us all feel human again. We weren't in a grey, faceless machine: we were humans, being dealt with by humans and by humans who cared and were prepared to show their caring. The next action emphasised the point. There was a blood pressure meter fixed to the wall by the hospital bed. Our doctor took Jane's blood pressure and found that there was a slow leak in the machine itself. It was only a minor puncture, but clearly it had been there for some time. He got a new portable blood pressure meter and took Jane's blood pressure with it. When he had noted that down, he then said, 'There's no way this is going to get repaired unless it is properly broken'. With that he ripped the whole plastic tubing off the wall. The machine was now clearly broken. 'Now it will get mended', he said.

I don't know if he realised how significant that action was for Jane and me. We were worried that Jane was going to be submerged in a mechanical system. By demonstrating that he was prepared to subvert the system to get the right thing done, our doctor had shown that he was on our side and that we could trust him.

More about empowerment

Peter Block, in *The Empowered Manager*, relates these ideas of the little things to the specific issue of change. He says:

'Even if we are part of a major change effort, we are still faced with the individual problem of what we do this afternoon and first thing tomorrow morning. Lasting improvement does not take place by pronouncements or official programmes. Change takes place slowly inside each of us, and by the choices we think through in quiet, wakeful moments lying in bed just before dawn. Culture is changed not so much by

[124]

carefully planned, dramatic and visible events as by each of us focusing on our own action in the small, barely noticed, day to day activities of our work. In a way, the only culture that exists for us is the room in which we are standing at the moment. It is the transformation of the culture of the room we are in that holds the possibility of transforming the culture of the rest of the organisation. It is change from the inside out.'

In other words, when we each focus on the little things of the present and become living examples of the organisation we wish to see created, the larger change process has already begun. Sometimes the little things that make a difference occur in the area earlier described as constructive disobedience.

Successful disobedience

Edgar recalls working in an office where once a month two solid days were spent in allocating the costs of the work by a large fleet of lorries, vans and cars. The normal method was to sort the log sheets of the drivers into date order and then transcribe each journey by its number of miles under a cost heading, adding them up at the end of the month's sheets. This would be done for, say, some thirty vehicles and there were, in the department, some forty people, each dealing with their thirty vehicles. At the end of each vehicle record, the miles were turned into money. It took about two days altogether.

Edgar noticed that, in the main, each vehicle only attended to one cost heading, say services overhead, services underground, retail sales, etc. He therefore took the first mileage from the last, pulled out any exception and that vehicle was done. He finished the job in two hours, whereupon the immediate supervisor was greatly perturbed to hear how he had finished the job so quickly and insisted that it be done 'properly', in 'the way that we have always done it' – typical words often heard when change is broached. To cut a long story short, a series of more senior supervisors and ultimately the big boss were called in because Edgar refused to do as he had been told. The big boss listened: 'What is this I hear? You not doing as you're told,

Wille?' He listened again and said, 'Well, look, we'll leave it for the moment and I'll think about this'.

The end of the story was that next month Edgar did the allocations of the transport to cost headings for the whole department in two or three days. A little thing, of no great consequence, but a significant saving in time and money. The moral is to be prepared to take the risk, for significant changes come from quite small beginnings. The next step in that department was computerisation, when forty people became three for the whole activity.

Your list of 'little things'

We now leave a section blank for you to participate and write here, or in that exercise book you've been using, a list of little things that you or anybody else could carry out in your department or organisation, which together would make, if not a big difference, at least a worthwhile one. We will do the same and we ask you to read ours *after* you've done your own.

Our list of little things

We have come up with a list of little things that would make a big difference. We have concentrated quite deliberately on actions that look almost ridiculously little – some of them are just part of good manners or common sense. Together they constitute a major change programme.

- Open the door for the catering person carrying a loaded tray.
- Report a light not working (and preventing a fire perhaps?).
- Turn the photocopying paper to face the right way in its pile, so that others may use it without problems.
- Remember the computer has been left on, and go all the way back from the car park to switch it off.
- Say 'please' and 'thank you' as if you mean it.
- Sandwich an adverse criticism between two pieces of praise.
- Give the extra five minutes.
- Be on time for that meeting.
- Make time to hear a colleague's problem, even when you're in a hurry.
- The odd encouraging remark, in passing, which can change a life. (Edgar remembers one: a month into a new job and his boss asked him about his aspirations. Edgar replied he wanted to have reached a certain stage before he was forty. The boss said: 'Good heavens, man, you'll be there long before you're forty.' Edgar was, and that little conversation was the turning-point).
- Timely reporting of a likely bottleneck.
- Make a note of that message and pass it on.
- Always have a pencil and notebook with you – to jot down ideas, before they go, or to make a note of what others are asking of you.
- Throw away papers no longer required (I don't always practise what I preach – EW).
- Notice worn tread on steps and get something done about it.
- Be gently suspicious of people hanging about where you wouldn't expect them to be.

- Report everything that isn't as it should be, however small, from the diminishing toilet roll to the cracked window, from the loose guttering to the hole in the path.
- Print key words in a message if you really can't write legibly.
- Return what you borrow – books or tools – and promptly.
- Ask always: 'How would I like to be at the receiving end of this behaviour?' or 'What does it feel like to be in that person's shoes?' (Those two questions could revolutionise the world, let alone the workplace.)
- Smile.
- Really find time to welcome new staff and give them a clear picture of what it's all about.
- Make sure someone knows where you are.
- Return telephone calls promptly.
- Look people in the eye.
- Think about the tone of your voice.
- Know the difference between preference and necessity (perhaps that's not a little thing).
- Congratulate people on personal successes or special achievements.
- Reduce the time taken to perform a task by five seconds.
- Reduce the distance to be reached for an article by twelve inches.
- Have everything at the right height.
- Listen with interest.
- Make your written sentences shorter.
- Think of the recipient of your work as your customer.

.... and thousands more.

'It depends on me'

The themes of Chapters 9, 'More power than you think you have', and this one, 'The little things that make a big difference', link with Peter Block's six points under the heading 'The Commitment We Make to Ourselves':

1. We are the architect of the organisation choosing its form and future. We are not just a labourer following another's plans.

2. We set goals that are unique and that no one else has achieved before in *exactly* the same way.
3. We choose the path of high resistance and live with the anxiety which that creates.
4. We risk all we have – not for the thrill of it, but because there is no safe path.
5. We are the place of last resort. There is no one to take care of us.
6. We are responsible for problems; if we don't handle them, no one will.

These maxims may sound as if Block has given up his hope of anything approaching Harrison's love in the workplace, but even though we believe in that, we have to realise that we are responsible for ourselves and that 'it depends on me'. Then things can begin to happen.

Note to reader as co-author
Add here examples of little things you or colleagues have done which made a difference.

_____

_____

_____

_____

_____

_____

_____

_____

_____

_____

_____

_____

_____

_____

_____

_____

_____

_____

_____

_____

_____

_____

_____

_____

_____

_____

_____

_____

Chapter 11

HARNESSING EVERYONE'S ENERGY

The previous two chapters have considered approaches which will influence the implementation of change – approaches which recognise our own power to affect the course of affairs and which see major changes as being derived from a host of little actions. We have looked at some of the skills required.

We now proceed to bring together some of the other skills needed by organisations and individuals to achieve effective and beneficial change. Not surprisingly, many of them are concerned with how to win support from others for desirable changes, even though they may at first appear unwelcome. These largely depend upon understanding the feeling side of human make-up. Other skills are more cognitive and rational.

Let us suppose that only you and one or two others know about a change that you are proposing. It is now time to share the secret with others who may be affected by the process. All you have to do is harness their minds and hearts. Easily said, but not so easily done. The main reason for the difficulty is that we often assume that the mind and reason should suffice. We do not give sufficient emphasis to the power of emotion.

Managers may be quite good at presenting the logic of their change proposals, and people may even respond to the logic and see that it all makes good sense, yet emotional acceptance may be lacking. If that is the case, acceptance will not be wholehearted. (The last word says it all: the heart has to be receptive.) We have to nurture the emotional readiness for change, as well as showing the rational need for it.

When people are asked to change in some respect, they will be required to modify some way of doing things, to learn new

[132]

skills and approaches. They will probably then feel less skilled than they previously did. They may feel a threat to the competence which they hitherto felt they had. (Even as I type, I am experiencing that feeling; I have been asked by one of our assistants, who is doing most of the typing, to conform to the proper two spaces before a new sentence. Not being a proper typist, I've only ever left one, and having to think about this change is cramping my style.) To handle emotional resistance successfully calls for some understanding about how people learn skills.

The stages of learning new skills

Think back to the time before you learned to drive a car. Phil's son, who is nine, knows that it is very easy to drive a car: you just move the steering wheel, tread on the accelerator, do things with the gears and the car goes along. 'Go faster, Dad, go faster', 'come on, overtake this car.' He doesn't realise that a bus is coming or that it would be unsafe in some other way. He is at the first stage of skill acquisition as far as driving a car is concerned (see Figure 11.1). He is at the stage of *unconscious incompetence*.

Now think back to the time when you first sat in a car. You looked down at your feet and saw that there were two feet and three pedals, which was fairly daunting! Gradually you learned to make the car go forward and backward when you wanted it to, and with considerable effort you learned to manoeuvre it. You were at the stage of *conscious incompetence*.

Gradually you became more competent at controlling the car, you moved into heavier traffic, you took on more difficult junctions and traffic conditions, and you learned about road sense as well. The car now did what you wanted, but it took a lot of concentration. You were at the stage of *conscious competence*. Most people seem to take their driving test at this stage. That's why it is usually such a nerve-racking experience.

Then, after you have passed your driving test, you go on to drive a lot more, and now, if you are an experienced driver, you are able to drive along while listening to the radio, perhaps having a conversation with someone else and having the time to

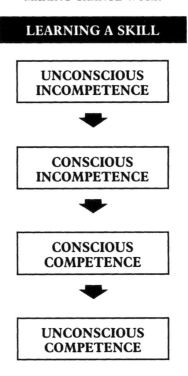

FIG. 11.1   The stages of learning new skills

notice that a new building is being put up on the corner of a street. You have reached the stage of *unconscious competence*. You have developed an auto-pilot kind of skill. Indeed, so automatic are these skills that we may have the experience of driving while holding an intense conversation with someone, and not being aware that we are driving at all. You find yourself automatically turning into the staff car park, because the route of your trip took you past your organisation's front door, and your automatic pilot naturally took you into the staff car park.

When people are being asked to change, they have to come off automatic pilot. Their regular pattern of behaviour is disturbed. They go back from the unconscious competent stage, at least to their conscious incompetent stage.

Most of us have had the experience of having to relearn a skill at some stage in our lives. For instance, anybody who has broken a leg and has had it in plaster for a few months will have had to relearn walking. Those of us with children have to relearn our helping role as their homework gets harder and outside our own range.

At work we like to think of ourselves as being competent, and we all much prefer to be effortlessly or unconsciously competent rather than have to work hard at it all the time. One of the major sources of resistance to change is people's unwillingness to be pushed back into conscious incompetence.

Owning change

In a change situation it is too easy to assume the role of victim. In fact people become quite skilled at being victims. But you can't remain a victim *and* take on ownership of a change. How do you get people to take ownership?

'Victimness' arises because people are fearful of the unknown. It is easier to blame some other person or authority for what has gone wrong than to face up to our own fears about what we know and what we don't know. A manager who tries to bring about change by bluff, saying that all is well and all will continue to be well, actually creates the environment in which victims can flourish. At the first sign that something is going wrong, the victims can turn and say: 'I told you so, it's all your fault'.

Getting people to take responsibility is a much more subtle process. It starts by recognising that although the unknown is there, it can be limited to a specific area. If we all know what is not known, then at least that limits speculation about what other nasty things are round the corner.

Ownership increases, too, when personal power and effectiveness increase; most people have more power in change situations than they believe. An example to add to those in Chapters 9 and 10 illustrates this. On an overseas consultancy assignment Phil was faced with a group of managers who were saying that they were powerless to act because of government legislation. He challenged them to find even small things that they could do that would make a difference. A morning of brainstorming produced several actions, some of which were achieved before lunchtime. Although in themselves trivial, these actions allowed the managers to recognise that they had power, that they could have an effect, and that a small effect could lead to a larger one in progressive leaps and bounds.

Our twin themes of 'more power than you think you have' and 'the little things that make a big difference' are crucial to creating readiness for change and ownership of it among stakeholders. You can't bring about most major changes in a short while, but you can give people some clues and some encouragement. Perceptive selection of little things that can be acted on straight away will send signals throughout the organisation that change is possible, and possible at *my* level too. When everyone at whatever level in the organisation starts reporting what they *can* do to make that change happen, then the process is really under way. While it is still perceived as owned only by the top management or the change project team, then the change has not really started.

Change and culture

In change situations within a company there are the twin strands of logical task-oriented activity and the broader, fuzzier band of its culture. It is fairly simple to instruct people to work on new tasks and to set up the necessary rules and systems to make those tasks happen; it is much harder to change the cultural style of the company. It can be relatively easy to move to a stage where the tasks have changed but the culture hasn't, but those tasks will easily revert to the previous norm because the culture hasn't changed. The ideal is for the culture to move, and then the new tasks can be worked at in a new atmosphere. How can you move the culture?

Firstly, recognise that changing tasks will not produce real change. In Chapter 6 we saw how Larry Greiner identified five crises where there is some kind of revolution in the company's operation; between each revolution there is a period of evolutionary growth. It is worth looking at his model in greater depth as a help in relating change initiatives to the stage of an organisation's evolution.

When the company is young, growth through creativity is usually identified with one or a few individuals who are putting an idea into practice. The idea takes off and more people are employed by the organisation. At some stage there will be a crisis of leadership. Can one person control all the many people and things that are now going on under that name. To survive this first crisis the organisation needs to appoint a strong business manager, who may not necessarily have much specific knowledge about the original creative idea on which the organisation was founded.

In the second growth phase the organisation becomes functionally efficient, accounting systems are created, communications become formalised and a power structure is set up. This leads to a crisis of autonomy, when staff at lower levels feel restricted by the centralised structure. They have developed knowledge about markets and processes which are not known at the top level. These lower level staff know that they are ready for more responsibility.

If they win their point, then the company moves into the third stage – delegation. Greater responsibility is passed down, and very often the organisation splits into a decentralised operation. This leads to the next crisis point – control. It is not possible for the management team to keep in touch with all the activities being run in its name. Some top managements try to recentralise management. Others are prepared to allow decentralised structures to continue. Either way the whole organisation needs co-ordination rather than control at this stage. Everyone needs to be aligned to the same aim and the same vision.

We then move into the fourth phase of growth through co-ordination, which can be very productive. Increasing emphasis is placed on the development of staff. Human resources personnel are hired and some benefits of specialisation are gained. Eventually, however, a fourth crisis of red tape occurs. Here, so much co-ordination is happening that there is little time to get on with the work. At least, that is how they see it down on the shop floor and at divisional or unit levels.

The fifth and last observable phase is growth through collaboration. Many organisations have learned to operate in a collaborative way, and this has been very beneficial. The focus is on solving problems through team action, rather than implementing one person's specific view. We have given examples of this in Chapter 8. People are assembled into teams depending on the need of the task rather than status or authority. No doubt, however, the sequence of crisis and evolution continues beyond phase 5.

Change and individual trauma

In the same way that organisations go through predictable stages of growth and development, so do individuals. We can learn here from those who have experience in counselling the bereaved. Bereavement is probably the most dramatic change that people have to come to terms with. Faced with it, people's behaviour goes through very clear stages. We also go through similar stages in much less traumatic circumstances. We go through the transitions described below in order to come to terms with the new state of affairs. It is also possible to get stuck at several of the stages, which can be a major source of resistance to change.

SELF-ESTEEM CHANGES DURING TRANSITIONS

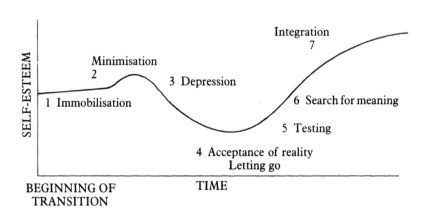

FIG. 11.2 Self-esteem changes during transitions, based on Adams, Hayes & Hopson (1976) *Towards an understanding of transition, Understanding and Managing Personal Change*

[138]

The first stage a person goes through when given some new and traumatic information is that of immobilisation. When given bad news, we tend to freeze. It may be a physical freezing, where we are almost paralysed, or it can just be a mental freezing. The immobilisation can be felt as a sense of incompetence and of powerlessness.

The next stage is to deny that the change has occurred. We will minimise the information that has been given or even deny it. People often say 'It can't be true', 'It can't be happening to me'. We can get stuck at this stage. There are a few tragic cases of people who have never truly accepted that a change has occurred. We hear of people who have been made redundant, but still go to work every day because they cannot accept the reality of what has happened. Notice also that self-esteem has increased with the denial of the change. If the change is denied, then of course our self-esteem can rise because we believe there is nothing to be concerned about.

Usually, however, this stage moves fairly quickly into the longer phase of depression. When people become aware of what has actually happened, they get depressed; their energy levels fall, their physical appearance may change slightly, and their confidence go down dramatically. This ties in with a drop in self-esteem. Unfortunately, many people quite enjoy being depressed and can get stuck at the depression stage. We have talked about being the victim of change; by being depressed, the victim can find a permanent way of life.

Some people never get out of the depression phase. If they do, it is because they begin to accept the reality of what has happened. It is always a painful time to accept that the world will never be quite the same as it was before. However, people are able to do this and to let go of the past. Counselling at this stage can help an individual to learn to let go. Once they have done that, they then start to assess how they will behave in future.

Once people have accepted that the world will never be the same again, then new opportunities may present themselves. There is then a period of testing out new behaviours, new attitudes, new ways of behaving. This can be quite alarming for the friends and colleagues of, say, a 45-year-old man who, having gone through some major change, behaves for a while as if he were a teenager. What he is doing is testing out a whole range of new behaviours which were never feasible before, but might just work in this new situation. Once these ideas have been tested, they are then given some kind of meaning. We all like to feel that what we do has some meaning. The move from almost random testing of behaviours into something that is meaningful to the individual happens at this stage.

The final stage is the integration of these new behaviours and their meaning into the individual's life as a whole. Many parts of their behaviour continue outwardly unchanged, but there is a new flavour to life.

For people who are going through a major change personally, the need to be allowed some freedom to test and explore new behaviours is very important. Some people report that they are held back from making the changes they wish to make by the pressure of friends and colleagues who want them to stay the same. In a sense, the friends and colleagues have not accepted that the world has changed and is different for these persons and want to see them in their old style, in their old ways. These pressures can be quite intense.

Note to reader as co-author
Add here an example of a traumatic change from which you nevertheless recovered.

_____

_____

_____

_____

_____

_____

_____

_____

_____

_____

_____

_____

_____

_____

_____

_____

_____

_____

_____

_____

_____

_____

_____

Chapter 12

RESISTANCE TO CHANGE

In Chapter 11 we considered how to release energy for change
by dealing positively with people's feelings, such as the sense of
incompetence which they often feel when required to change;
by recognising the impact of organisational culture upon
change situations; and by dealing empathetically with the sense
of loss many people experience when 'bereaved' of the familiar
ways. In this chapter we move on to more specific causes of
resistance to change, apart from the broad issues we have
considered. What is it that causes people to block proposals and
get in the way of 'progress'?

Sometimes it is lack of understanding about what the changes
will mean. Sometimes it is fear of those changes and the implications for the person concerned. In many cases the fear is a fear
of the unknown. A very useful way of analysing resistance to
change has been developed by our colleagues at Ashridge, Bill
Critchley and David Casey. They have identified five patterns
of believing, feeling and behaving which may cause resistance
to change. They have also identified possibilities for working
with these resistant patterns – rigidity, overreaction, 'yes–but',
suspicion, and action orientation.

Rigidity

People who are concerned with security, procedures and rules
will say it is the 'right' way to do something, and they are
inflexible about changing this or that rule. They operate from a
purely logical point of view, and don't believe they can show

their emotions or use their intuitions or even express a view at a meeting without checking first that it is correct. This is likely to be a defence against anxiety and against a show of feelings. Their colleagues regard these people as having left their hearts in the car park when they come into work each morning.

To cope with this kind of resistance to change it is necessary to demonstrate to them in a very logical fashion the long-term consequences of their behaviour. An emotional argument will not succeed, but a logical argument might. We have to understand that they find great comfort in knowing the rules and the system, and sticking with them. Such people will hang on to their rules and systems for as long as possible, because they represent stability in an unstable world.

Overreaction

In the kind of organisations where people overreact, drama and crisis are the norm. In many ways this is the opposite of the situation where rigidity prevails. This tendency towards organisational hysteria is usually a defence against true information and logical use of it to solve the problem. Some managers enjoy living in permanent crisis, because crisis management is the only kind of management they know and understand. It is easy to get so wound up in the excitement of the crisis that logical thought and rational evaluation of new data are not possible. There is no time because of the crisis. People who feel comfortable in displaying their emotions are drawn to this kind of organisation, living on a permanent kind of stage, giving marvellous performances, but never getting anywhere.

The technique for handling this type of reaction is to empathise with them and help them in the process of solving the problem for themselves. A major mistake would be to solve the problems for them. This kind of person is delighted to off-load problem-solving on to anybody else who will take it on. If they are allowed to get away with this, they will never actually implement a solution themselves, because naturally they are having a crisis and they have no time. (Some of our examples in Chapter 8 looked to managers to help their staff solve their own problems.)

[143]

'Yes–but'

The third pattern is where everyone knows the problem and has thought about it in some depth. But no one wants to take responsibility for making anything happen. No one seriously wants to take ownership of the problem that has been identifed. It is easier to blame someone upwards, sideways or downwards rather than to take action yourself. People create a classic victim culture and therefore find themselves unable to move. They spend most of their energy blaming others rather than moving forwards. Whatever solutions emerge, there is always a 'Yes–but'.

The way to handle these people is to confront what, in essence, is passive behaviour. They know that the problem exists, but they expect others to solve it. Then from a safe position they can criticise the solution as not good enough. People need to move in order to create the conditions in which a solution will work. It is a classic case of people having more power than they realise, but they can be brought to accept the fact.

A colleague of ours worked with an organisation recently which was claiming to be stuck on a change process. In going round and talking to a variety of staff, he was told that what he was doing seemed very similar to a study that had been done five years previously. When he asked for and got hold of the details, from five years ago, it demonstrated that almost identical data was being discovered and almost identical problems were being faced then! The company had failed to move forward at all in the intervening five years.

Our colleague confronted the senior management of that organisation with this failure to move, or even to use the data that was available, and brought them to the realisation that there were things they could do that would help them move from their present position. But they had to take responsibility for those actions, and accept that they would make mistakes in their choices. Our colleague refused to enter into debates about what the best solution would be, because he realised that the members of the company were far more knowledgeable about the problem than he was. They could always out-argue him as to why they shouldn't change. The only thing to do was to take the organisation by the scruff of the neck and get it to do something, almost anything.

Suspicion

Where this prevails, there is a kind of organisational paranoia. Managers and employers spend their time protecting their own patch, protecting their own back, and scoring points off others. The organisation is characterised by chronically low levels of trust. This approach is usually a defence against the belief that 'someone will get you if you don't watch out'.

Action orientation

For some people action seems to be the best defence against thinking. Companies get obsessed with work, short-term results, and tasks being done – any action so long as everyone's busy! All the energy of the organisation is concerned with what you do rather than why you do it. It is in this kind of organisation that people do things right rather than do the right things. Then, combined with a need for rules and systems, this can be a most formidable organisation. In the short term it will probably be very effective because of its energy levels. In the long term it may chase off down a blind alley way and become completely marooned. This kind of organisation can become obsessed with its own short-term success, and believe that to do better you have to work harder, not smarter.

The strategy for helping to deal with this blockage is first to review the way things are done – the why not the what – and ask people about their purpose and mission. What actually do they get out of their work? Why do they need to be so busy? These are usually difficult and painful questions to be asked, and it will be easy to brush them off as irrelevant. There is always the pressure of more tasks and more activity. The short-term success of this kind of organisation is always a good excuse for not reviewing the longer-term performance as well. Eli Goldratt (1984) has shown how concern to have everyone busy all the time in production situations can create serious bottlenecks.

[145]

Overcoming the resistance

The single biggest problem in all these behaviour patterns is
fear of the unknown. We would like to offer some approaches to
helping people overcome this fear.

The hologram

The first is what we describe as the hologram effect. Using laser
light, a holographic image can be created on photographic film.
When the film is illuminated, it will give the appearance of a
three-dimensional object. With conventional film, taking a
small fraction of the negative gives you a small fraction of the
picture, but with the hologram, a small fraction of the negative
can still produce the whole picture. On the hologram, each part
of the negative contains data about the whole image. We believe
there is an analogy to be drawn between the hologram and a
change process in an organisation. If you are operating at the
two levels of task and culture, then if the change process is
going well, it should be possible to take even a small fraction of
the organisation and see in it examples of the change process as
it affects the whole organisation.

As an example of this, take an engineering company that Phil
worked with recently. It was seeking to move from being
product-centred to customer-centred. All sorts of initiatives
were taken to ensure that the design of new products was based
on market needs rather than on engineering design. The products were complex and took a long time to redesign. How
could a visiting executive from head office check that this
customer-centred orientation was really working? Obviously it
would be easy to look at the new designs and check with some
key customers, and of course this should be done. But each part
of the organisation should reflect the new customer orientation
if the change was truly company-wide. Why not ask in the
canteen?

In our example that is exactly what the visiting executive did.
He discovered that since the change process was initiated,
design engineers had been coming into lunch not at the usual
one o'clock all in a group, but had been staggering their times of
coming to lunch. The canteen had been irritated by this at first,
but had gradually accommodated itself to it. The canteen

supervisor enquired why it was happening and was told by design engineers that they got many phone calls during the lunchtime from their customers, and they now wished always to have two of their colleagues at their desks ready to take calls at this period. It was proving to be a very useful opportunity to hear about customer needs that would otherwise be missed.

Listening to criticism

Of course, these engineers had discovered one other principle of avoiding blockages to change, which is very simple to describe but very hard to do. They had discovered the benefits of listening to criticism. Unfortunately in many organisations the top management have created subtle and not so subtle structures which make it almost impossible for bad news ever to get to the top. If the messenger always gets shot, then eventually the company will run out of messengers willing to take on the job of bringing the bad news to the chairman. The chairman then only hears good news and of course believes that all is going well. He neither appreciates that there is a need for change nor does his readiness for change alter in any significant way. It is a version of the story of the emperor's new clothes, and has been played out in countless organisations over the last few decades.

How do you get people to tell you bad news? A recent study of effective versus ineffective managers showed that one of the features of effective managers was that they seldom surprised their bosses. They had found a way of communicating the ups and downs of their work so that they seldom brought surprise or shock. Managers who were criticised by their subordinates and their bosses were the ones who delayed telling them that things were going badly, or even concealed the bad news because they felt they would be blamed. They failed to realise that it looks even worse the longer you conceal it.

Risk-taking

But setbacks and failures are of themselves a healthy part of change management. Thomas J. Watson, the founder of IBM, said the way to succeed is to double your failure rates. Not being afraid of failure is probably the key emotional strength that change managers need to have. Any fundamental change calls for doing things differently, and this means risk, and failure sometimes. The effective change manager is not put off by the failure. Indeed he/she learns from it. A study of ninety top leaders by Warren Bennis showed that while all of them recognised they had made mistakes, some of which were catastrophic, none of them regarded themselves as having failed completely. There was always something each of them could learn from any catastrophe. Positive failure and the strength to recover and move forward seem to be essential features of good change management.

Of course, it helps if the organisation is structured in such a way that risk-taking and consequent failure are not punished. Phil once worked with an organisation that on average set ten targets for each manager, on which their bonus and incentive payments were based. Until quite recently the manager had to hit all ten targets before the bonus was paid. Even if the manager had exceeded some of the subtargets by 100 per cent or 200 per cent and in fact had a brilliant year, but had not hit all ten targets, there was no bonus. Over a period of time this approach tended to mean that managers would negotiate easy targets for themselves and would not take risks. Risk-taking was seen as unproductive and unrewarded, and gradually began to diminish in the company. A change of policy on incentive and bonus payments allowed risk-taking to be rewarded, and re-established an entrepreneurial approach at all levels of management.

Management of chaos

Most of us have been brought up in an era where science has dominated. Science provides the logical analysis of data and the ability to predict outcomes for the future. In running a business, many of us have been led to believe that if only we could get sufficient data and apply the correct rules to that data, we would be able to predict the outcomes of our decisions. Sophisticated techniques have been created to help predict what will happen and to ensure decisions are made at the right time.

[148]

Project management is a science in itself and is quite well understood. Companies use budgets as planning tools and rolling five-year strategy programmes as ways of keeping track of their progress and ensuring that they are on course. These techniques are very logical ones, and make the assumption of predictability. In recent years, however, a new facet of science has emerged – that of understanding chaos. Some systems, it appears now, are inherently unpredictable. No matter how much data you have, there will never be enough and it will never be detailed enough to predict how a system will operate. Examples abound in the natural world: the shape and development of clouds, the variations in leaves and snowflakes, the turbulence of smoke or of water going through rapids, to name a few. All these systems, all these shapes, mathematicians describe as fractals. The pattern appears similar, but it is impossible to predict precisely how the pattern will emerge. Weather systems fall into this category as well. They are frequently unpredictable in anything other than the very short-term.

Our hypothesis is that organisation systems are similar to weather systems. There are certain fractal patterns which can be identified, but not precisely predicted. In conventional science we have been led to believe that, for instance, if you know the muzzle velocity, the angle of the gun and the wind speed, then it is possible to calculate the landing point of the shell. We tend to believe that if we have the right data, we can make predictions of where every kind of shell will land. A weather system is not like this; in order to cope with the weather, we must have a certain level of resourcefulness. If we wish to stay warm and dry on a day in late October, in Northern Europe, we must expect to carry clothing and perhaps umbrellas in order to protect us from the *possibility* that it may rain or that it may even snow. If we were in the Sahara Desert, the need to carry an umbrella for protection from the rain would be much less! It might be useful as a sunshade, though. Handling risk is thus a matter of handling unpredictable systems.

A manager in a small accounts department wanted to install a new computer system. The present computer system was functionally very effective but was becoming overloaded by the number of accounts which had to be held and the requests for special analyses from head office. With his two accounts supervisors he reviewed possible software and hardware options. He took advice from the computer people at head office and came to a decision which pleased everyone. He arranged for his staff to be trained in the new software and in new operating procedures. He organised a period of parallel running, where the old system was maintained alongside the new. This put tremendous strain on all the employees, but they recognised the importance of not losing their old data base before they had become thoroughly familiar with the new one.

When it was felt that the new system was coping, and anyway everyone was getting exhausted by trying to run two systems in parallel, all work was transferred to the new system. It ran successfully for the first week, and the manager, very tired from all the overtime and weekend working he had done, went away on holiday. He returned ten days later to a desk that had never been more full of paper and to an office staff who were clearly in a very low state of morale. What had gone wrong? Why were the supervisors now arguing with each other, and blaming their staff for being incompetent and not caring about the new system?

The manager spent time with each of these supervisors, and each of the other staff in the office. He learned that most of the time the new system was a considerable improvement on the old. But there were occasions when special actions had to be taken, and special instructions were needed. No one felt they had the expertise to authorise these special instructions. Hence the staff and supervisors were trying to force every situation into the normal working pattern. Of course it was not succeeding.

But why had no one raised these issues with the manager before he went on holiday? Surely some instances had occurred during the parallel running time? Of course they had, he was told, but they were busy keeping the two systems running and they didn't want to show their ignorance: so they never came and told him. The manager had planned the implementation of the new system in all its logical detail and had correctly anticipated all the logical problems that might arise. However, he had not anticipated – and we would argue could never have anticipated – all the possible emotional and non-logical problems that might arise.

He could have made provision for coping with this kind of problem, in the same way that we make provision for a sudden shower of rain by taking an umbrella. He could have allowed time for his staff to come and talk to him during the implementation period and after the parallel running period. He could even have deliberately gone and spoken to each of the participants in the new system and asked them about their own personal responses to it, rather than whether they were achieving the tasks set. The man was a good planner in a logical sense, but he was not planning his resourcefulness to cope with unforeseen events.

The more we move our organisation into periods of fundamental change, the more we are managing chaos. Those of us who prefer the comfort of precise prediction either have to leave now or reject the old predictive way in favour of the new flexibility, which adapts to the new and the unexpected.

Chapter 13

CHANGE SKILLS

We have looked at how to cope with people's feelings about change and with their patterns of behaviour when faced with it. We now turn to some specific skills which help in handling change. We take for granted the normal management skills of planning, co-ordination, control, delegation etc., with the proviso that, by its very nature, change tends to play havoc with traditional approaches. Nevertheless, you can't manage change if you can't manage anything else.

In this chapter we pick out a few other skills that have special relevance for managers seeking to bring about change or to incorporate it into their work.

There is also an important distinction to be made between leadership and management. Adapting one of Peter Drucker's sayings, Warren Bennis argues that management is about doing things right and leadership is about doing the right things. He comments from a study in America that many companies are overmanaged but underled. Clearly, the component of leadership skills is an important one in any change management process.

The skills listed below have been identified in people who appeared competent at managing change, whether initiated by themselves or by others.

Reframing

Reframing is putting an existing idea into a new context or framework. We already think of turning problems into oppor-

[152]

tunities and how every cloud has a silver lining. Reframing is no more than doing that as a mental habit. When Jan Carlzon said that Scandinavian Airlines was not a collection of aeroplanes and equipment, but was 50 million moments of truth (a moment of truth being every time a member of staff met a customer or potential customer), he was reframing the context in which people thought of the airline. The reframing in itself did nothing except create the possibility for other changes to occur.

He also neatly inverted the classic structure of the hierarchy and put himself as chief executive at the bottom, thus showing that he saw himself as supporting all the managers and customer contact staff, who, he said, were the keys to the company's success. Again, nothing changed directly as a result of this, but opportunities were opened that were not opened before.

If you like party games, you might like to draw four lines through the nine dots in Figure 13.1, without lifting the pen from the paper and without going through any dot more than once. The solution in Figure 13.2 is well known, but illustrates the point. If you think of the nine dots as contained in the frame of a square, you will not get there. The solution will only come by getting outside the natural frame of the dots.

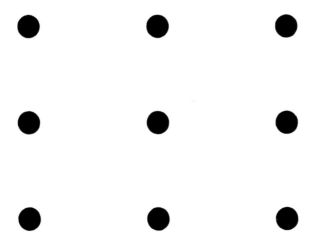

FIG. 13.1   Reframing problem

[153]

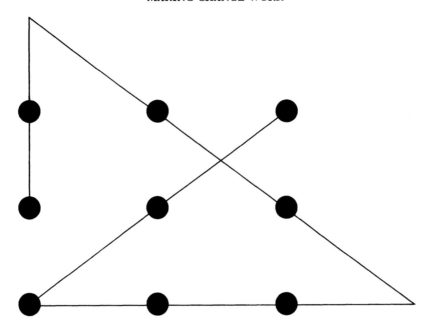

FIG. 13.2   Solution to reframing problem

Watzlawick and his associates (1974) tell a story about a man with a stutter who wished to become a salesman. He feels at first that his impediment will prevent him from being a good sales person. Surely salesmen are slick and have clever ways of talking people into buying things they don't want? But then he is encouraged to remember that this style of approach often irritates many customers. What do most people do when faced with a stutter? They listen, answer and they help out. What would most salesmen love their customers to do? Answer: listen and help out. The man went on to be a brilliant salesman because he had reframed an impediment into an advantage.

We have noticed that change managers are continually reframing every problem, every idea, every piece of data. It becomes a mental habit, so that opportunities are seldom missed.

Reframing can also help when fear of change or of failure is rocking a person. Imagine that you are asked to walk along a

[154]

one metre-high wall which is one metre wide. My guess is that you would be able to do it fairly easily. Now make the wall twenty metres high. It would be harder to walk along that same wall, wouldn't it? If you could now reframe, in your own mind, the wall back down to one metre high, you could still walk along it. You would have to have reframed so perfectly that you truly believed that the wall was only one metre high.

A great tightrope walker quoted by Warren Bennis, the Great Walenda, said that, 'Walking on the tightrope is living, everything else is just waiting'. That is true reframing on an epic scale. It allowed the man to accomplish amazing feats, because he had reframed his world. The day he forgot it, he fell and died.

Reframing seems to have great potential benefits in that it opens up opportunities. But on its own it is not enough.

Zooming

We have all heard of taking the helicopter view: taking a wide perspective of all the aspects of some process or activity. We believe that is not enough. Effective change managers must not just take the helicopter's wide-angle perspective, but on occasion zoom in to look at the detail and check that it fits with the company plan.

A hotel manager concerned with changing the market in which his hotel operates may wish to zoom in on precisely what impression the arriving guest has of the hotel. What does the lobby look like, what lighting levels are appropriate, is the carpet plain or patterned, etc.? Most of these details will be handled by more junior staff, but the change manager will want to sample some of the minute details as experienced by the customer or the client in order to test whether they fit with the plan. In this way the manager is zooming in and out between very detailed close-ups and wide-angle pictures of the whole scene.

Clearly a manager who has not come to terms with delegating most of the work would be incompetent at zooming. Detailed work, particularly for task-orientated managers, is very attractive. Trying to zoom when you have not mastered delegation

[155]

will just result in you adding a heap of detailed work to your own workload. Subordinates then begin to lose interest as the manager takes over their own work and responsibilities for them. The change process is being halted and even reversed, because one person is taking too much of the work on himself or herself.

A nice story is told of Lord Laing, until recently the chairman of United Biscuits. From time to time, he would go out with his van drivers as an assistant. He would travel in the cab and take on whatever responsibilities the assistant normally had on that day. He tells a number of amusing stories of how he managed to lose papers or in other ways got things wrong. But all the time he was doing this, he was also learning about one aspect of one detail of the company's operation. By sampling life from a delivery driver's point of view, Lord Laing was zooming in on what he regarded as an important aspect of the company's work. As a spin-off, he was also demonstrating to his delivery drivers that he was prepared to work with them rather than be the 'big boss' operating at a distance.

In their frequently quoted book *In Search of Excellence*, Peters and Waterman describe this way of operating as 'managing by wandering about'. From the outside the wandering can almost seem aimless, and certainly chance plays a part. However, the manager practising effective zooming will rapidly develop a sense of where to zoom and when. I once heard a policeman, in his final year before retirement, being asked how it was that he had caught more criminals that year than some of his younger, much more athletic, colleagues. The man replied with a grin that he knew which way a villain would run and so he put himself in the right place. His younger colleagues spent their time racing round after the criminal. 'It's much harder work that way,' he said.

Informal communication networks

If you bumped into one of your colleagues at work and he took you aside and told you with a serious look on his face that the company was getting into difficulties over a major contract, and he had heard that there were likely to be redundancies, yet when you got back to your desk, you found a memo from the chairman saying that all was well and there was no need to worry, whom would you believe? We have asked this question of a number of managers who have come on our own programmes and we have never heard anyone vote for the memo. Rumours, gossip, idle conversation are all wonderfully rich ways to send messages round an organisation.

Of course, we all use the formal methods of communication that occur within a business. We receive memos, we read notices, we see that company video, etc. However, in our experience, people take more notice of the informal communications that occur in a company, particularly over matters of major importance.

In the same way that the Brothers Grimm wrote cautionary tales to impress on children the right and wrong ways of conducting themselves, so in every organisation you will find cautionary tales which are told to every newcomer. It is the cautionary tales, and the myths and legends that are spread informally, that actually create the culture of the company. If these do not match up with the formal pronouncements, like vision statements and mission statements, we think people will believe what other people tell them rather than what they read on a memo. A rumour is worth a thousand memos in this business.

So the effective change manager must be plugged into a network of informal communications. As we said in Chapter 9, effective change managers take care to be part of many networks and to listen carefully to what those networks are telling them. In addition, the network can provide useful support and be a source of ideas. Like-minded people will be able to contribute to the change process, and will feel able to criticise without fear of retribution. They can help build ownership and identify minor problems before they become major ones.

Of course, creating and working in networks is a skill for which some people have greater aptitude than others. The managers who enjoy working on their own, who like being solo operators, will have greater difficulty here. The people who can be social and who can give and receive trust comfortably will find networking a lot easier. It really does help to do this if you like people.

One of us recently worked in an organisation where there were a number of regional managers. Two of these managers were of particular interest because one was a great technical expert, while his colleague was much better at networking but much less experienced on the technical side. The organisation was going through a huge change brought on by increased competition and a need to cut costs while improving service. Over the six-month period that we knew both managers we were fascinated by the very different methods that each used.

The technical man would frequently use his technical experience to make bold and imaginative decisions concerning new businesses he was searching for. However, when he became ill and was away from the office for nearly three weeks, most of his staff were unable to keep up the good work. They had relied on this technical expertise and his impressive knowledge to guide their business through the difficult times.

On the other hand, the second manager, who, although he had less technical knowledge and experience, was relying more on his other staff, built up a team of people who supported each other much more. This manager made a point of knowing what was going on everywhere in his region. He knew when people were having problems, and he knew when they were having successes. He always made sure that successes were recognised, and that everyone learnt from each success. He applied the same principle to learning from mistakes. But he always encouraged his staff to be creative. There were several occasions when a crisis loomed in his region, because an individual had made a poor decision. However, because his network was so wide-ranging, this second manager was always able to arrange support before things got out of hand.

The first manager was a great technician but didn't 'grow' his staff. They could try to copy him, but because their experience was generally less than his, they often felt frustrated that they could not do what he could do.

The second manager spent most of his time linking ideas and suggestions between staff. He said his job was to act as a kind of messenger.

In our view, the more technically competent manager will be most effective when life is fairly stable. In turbulent times, we believe that the networking manager is going to be more successful.

Parallel working

In many instances throughout this book, we have commented that change does not occur in a simple way; it usually occurs at several levels in several dimensions simultaneously. The effective change manager needs to find ways to operate on several fronts at once. It probably means cutting across functional and professional disciplines as well. Some organisations discourage this with a functional structure that expects managers to stay in one area of their greatest knowledge and not move out. The organisations best able to change encourage cross-functional activities and cross-functional groups. The change manager needs to be able to hold several threads of activity in his/her mind at once.

One of us recently spent some time working with a business development manager in a multi-national company. She was working in the computer and management services department, although freely admitted that she had very little computer technical background. However, much of the development of that particular part of the business was going to occur through the effective use of new technology, and so it was the right place for her to operate from. Her background had included work in a variety of different companies, operating in a variety of different markets and technologies.

Although we were talking about one particular change project, it was impressive to hear her draw on previous experience with other companies. As we dealt with each issue, she would ask questions. 'How will the technology people cope with that?' 'How will the personnel people implement their part of it?' 'How will we sell this to the main board?' She was processing the same issues through a number of different checklists. She recognised that what would work with the managing director would not be appropriate for one of the systems people. She considered the same issue but from a variety of different viewpoints.

When we came to the action planning part of our work, she was clear that a number of things had to occur at the same time for the change to work effectively. Her role during the time of implementation was split between the several strands we have been discussing.

[159]

Harnessing conflict

If someone disagrees with you, it is possible that they care just as much about the outcome of change as you, merely that they disagree on the methods being used. Effective change managers move towards objections of this sort because they recognise a source of energy. If they can find ways of harnessing that energy, they have an extra recruit to the campaign. The normal way of dealing with people who object to an idea of ours is to reject their proposals. We distance ourselves from them, either by criticising their ideas or by ignoring them. However, it is possible that when a person has the energy to object to your idea, their energy could be harnessed. We have noticed that change managers move towards areas of conflict and opposition, and very often manage to capture the energy that is being generated and harness it to the desired outcome. It is also part of the process of achieving ownership of the enterprise by the widest and largest number of people.

A professional colleague at a European business school was designing a new course for managers. The course was to be different in design and content from other courses put on by that business school. Our colleague's boss was not convinced that the new structure would be effective, or even that it was necessary to break away from a structure that had worked well for other courses.

Instead of retreating from the criticism of the boss, our colleague went out of his way to get closer to him and to understand his concerns and criticisms. We asked our colleague why he was doing this, since we also knew that in the business school he had enough freedom to put on the course without the full agreement of his own boss. His reply was that his boss represented many of the potential clients and users of the course he was designing. If he could not convince his boss that the structure of the programme was effective, then he knew he would have much greater difficulty in convincing potential clients for the programme. Thus it was to his advantage to understand his boss's objections to the structure of the programme, even though he knew he could, if he wished, push ahead with the original design.

As a postscript to this example, we learnt that his boss was

pleased to be a participant in the development of the programme and gave it considerable support from that point
onwards.

Idea connections

Whoever introduced Mr Rolls to Mr Royce was probably not
aware what a significant combination the two men would
become. Often there are part-ideas floating around an organisation which need to be joined up with other part-ideas. In this
way a new or improved product or process can emerge. Good
managers of change are always on the look out for part-ideas
that can be linked to other ideas. Often some reframing will be
necessary to convince one or other of the parties concerned that
it is worth spending some time with a person from an entirely
different functional discipline. However, the more linkages
that can be created, the more chance there is of a creative set of
solutions to the new problems.

A classic example of a linkage that produced enormous
profits is the 3M story of the post-it note. One of the staff was
presented with a sample of not very good glue. In a company
like 3M, which is known for its adhesive products, not very
good glue is hardly a star product. However, he had a particular
problem: he wished to keep markers in the pages of his hymn-
books when he sang at two different services each Sunday. He
found that ordinary slips of paper tended to fall out when he
turned the pages for one service and he wished them to stay in
position. He realised that not very good glue could be used to
keep the markers in place without damaging the surface of the
page in his hymn-book.

His ability to connect the use of not very good glue with the
need for removable book markers was the origin of the familiar
yellow 'post-its'. It took him a long time to develop a coating
process to put not very good glue on the surface of ordinary
paper, to create the 'post-it' note. It also took him a long time to
convince the marketing department, which was used to strong
stickiness, not weak stickiness, that not very good glue had
market potential. In the end, by delivering samples of post-it
notes to secretaries and referring their requests for more

supplies to the marketing department, he convinced the latter too.

Summary

Reframing – seeing existing things in a new way.

Zooming – dropping in close to the detail, but not staying there.

Networking – using informal communications to find out what's really happening and to enable you to harness the ideas of others.

Parallel working – being able to hold several threads in your hand at once.

Harnessing conflict – mobilising its energy instead of running away from it.

Idea connections – bringing together part-ideas from diverse sources to make new whole ones.

These are a few of the skills that will make change work.

Chapter 14

THE LEARNING ORGANISATION

This book began by considering the way in which change lies at the heart of individual human existence. We are all human becomings rather than just static human beings. Life is a process in which each microsecond hands on experience to the next microsecond, which reinterprets the whole chain of experience thus far and passes on something different to the next microsecond. So it goes on. Endless development, endless learning and endless change.

Then we added to that the recognition that human interactions continually change what we are, in similar fashion. Every time we interact with another human becoming, whether face to face or by reading or media attention, we are a marginally different person as a result of the encounter.

Thirdly, we put these concepts side by side with the Kolb learning cycle, where we have experiences, reflect upon them, draw out the principles and concepts we encounter and then act upon them in new situations.

So life for the individual is all a matter of change. Equally it is all about learning.

The individual is a learning organism. When individuals get together to act in concert, they become a learning organisation. The way in which they operate is a kind of expansion of the individual learning organism.

The collective perspective

Already we have seen how the individual is partly shaped as an individual by the relationship and interaction with other people. But we want to move on to see the collective version of this activity, where people deliberately seek a group identity and activity. It is this we are calling the learning organisation. It is this which has been mainly concerning us throughout this book.

There is something about a collective organisation of people which has an existence analogous to that of the individual. So real is this that we speak of the heart of the organisation, the spirit of the organisation, its soul, its values, its vision, its mission, its thought, its actions. When we do this, we are not just talking of the spirit, heart, actions of the chief executive or any one member of the organisation, but we are envisaging it as a whole, in which the whole is greater than the parts. We use the word 'synergy' to describe this power of the whole.

This approach does not minimise the role of the individual within the organisation, but neither does it isolate the individual from the whole collectivity.

Thus in this book, which is essentially concerned with organisational change, there has nevertheless been concern with the contribution of individual managers at all levels. So there has been emphasis on the fact that you, the individual manager or other employee, have more power to change things than you may think you have. We have talked about the little things that you can do, whoever you are, which can make a big difference, and we have given some examples. We have looked at triggers for change in organisations, and there we particularly saw the impact of the chief executive on the workings of the whole organisation. So the power of the individual is significant.

But we also saw, right from the beginning, that the individual is in a relationship with the other members of the organisation, and indeed with stakeholders, who may be outside the organisation but connected to it in some way or other. This came up first with the recognition that management is not only about mobilising resources, but also relationships.

It is the subtlety of these relationships which is the cement that binds people together into an organisation, rather than them being just a crowd.

Blending individual and group

Thus we have considered the changes out in the world in

general. As we did so, looking, for example, at a specimen of newspaper headlines, we had individual reactions, but also we were fitting these stories from the world outside into the perspective we shared with others as members of an organisation. *It* had interests with which we identified ourselves. Yet we also suggested that managers should encourage their staff individually to understand that world, to perceive fracture lines and future trends, so that they could be more effective, not only as individuals but also as members of the organisation.

The interaction between the individual and the collective perspective was also evident in the discussion of the future mindset. We suggested that decisions should be reached by projection of oneself and the group into the future and viewing the present from that perspective.

The blend of the individual and the collective is especially evident in the theme of the company life cycle, where the whole organisation and all the individuals comprising it go through a variety of stages. These stages are in fact the attempt to harmonise the individual and collective aspects of business activity. On the one hand, there is the attempt to maintain the individual creativity and the entrepreneurial spirit. But on the other hand, as life becomes more complex, and the interrelationships more difficult to link with smoothness, so system and bureaucratic methods get introduced to avoid a descent into anarchy, to be followed, one hopes, by a compromise to keep the best of both approaches.

The theme of change has in fact been dominated by a kind of seesaw between the individual and organisation concerns; by the learning which enables the individual to contribute, and the learning which happens within the organisation as a whole, whereby it progresses as a unique, though collective, entity. Nowhere was this more evident than in Chapter 8, where we shared some exciting stories of positive change in some British companies. Individuals took part in the changes of approach in Nissan, Rothmans, Ind Coope and other companies we mentioned. Their attitudes to work and to the company were changed, but the benefits came essentially to the group *as* a group and then to the individual through that medium. The key word was *team*, and it was through operating as teams that the

[165]

energies of individuals were liberated to contribute to something bigger than his or her own self.

It is this something bigger that we mean when we refer to the 'learning organisation'. Yes, the individual learns, but the team learns more on the basis of its synergy, where $1+1=3$ or more. The teams in the examples we cited were the means whereby discoveries were made, innovatory ideas tried out, and improvement continuously made (remember *kaizen* – continuous improvement). Feedback was received and shared, whether from the experiments made or from the reactions of the outside world; and listening to feedback and acting upon it is the essence of the learning organisation.

So this book has in practice had as its main theme the learning organisation in the very act of discussing change. If it results in more enterprises consciously equipping themselves so that they may become learning organisations, then our efforts will not have been in vain.

Learning through doing

We need to be clear that *the essence of a learning organisation lies in the doing of things*. It learns as it proceeds, as the teams comprising it act, in the practical carrying out of the purposes for which they have come together.

The organisation may be a place where learning in the cognitive sense is welcomed, where people are encouraged to go on courses to learn new skills or to gain new knowledge. This can certainly help the growth of the learning organisation, but it is not its essence. The learning organisation learns in and through the doing. It is the result of a collective and individual attitude to the job itself, where change, improvement, learning are key parts of the carrying out of the activity. Even the learning of new skills and knowledge is seen as part of the actual performance, rather than something added on from 'off the job'.

We felt that this book ought to end on this note of learning as a positive way of describing change. Most people welcome learning even if they are uncomfortable about change. By bringing the two ideas together in one pea pod we hope to enhance the cause of both. We are offering in this chapter a way of rereading everything which has gone before with another pair of spectacles, so that the earlier chapters can be enriched by an even wider perspective.

We would like to enlarge our understanding of the learning organisation by reference to one or two sources which have written about it, or in one case produced a video tape on the theme without even using the phrase.

The learning company

The definition of the learning company by Pedler, Boydell and Burgoyne in *MEAD* (1989) reflects concepts similar to those we have been discussing. They have a process which starts at the top, with organisational policy and strategy formation, evaluation and improvement consciously structured as a learning process. But this policy is not just handed down from the top. It is debated widely throughout the organisation, whose members are sharers, for whom recognition of differences, airing of disagreements, tolerating and working with conflicts are all part of the learning process by which decisions are reached.

In such companies, information flow and control systems in accounting, budgeting and reporting procedures are structured to assist learning from the consequences of management decisions, so that principles of future action can be derived, ('when we did this, then that happened'), as a means of doing better next time, not as an instrument of blame. All the feedback systems, whereby information is widely available, enable members to ask useful questions and gain material to aid individual and collective learning processes.

Moreover, such information becomes a resource which is shared across functions and departments, and it is constantly added to by those in the company with outside contacts, which enable them to act as environmental scanners for others as well as for their own purposes. There is furthermore in such companies a sense of freedom to share information with other stakeholders such as customers and suppliers.

Learning can come both from failures and from successes, but the latter spur on to yet further effort and do not merely breed complacency.

[167]

While the above points put the stress on collective and inter-active organisational learning, such companies will of course pay attention to individual learning and will tend to have a special emphasis on the self-development and self-managed learning approach. The Kolb learning model is relevant, both individually and collectively. You do things and have experiences, you reflect on them, and from this reflection principles of action emerge. These are then tested in action and enter the next part of the learning spiral. This is done collectively, and the reflection becomes constructive debate.

Transformation by learning

In some work they have done for the British Training Agency, Pedler, Boydell and Burgoyne define a learning company as 'an organisation which facilitates the learning of all members *and* continuously transforms itself'. They stress the importance of the two sides of this definition, to avoid the impression that a company which does a lot of training is thereby a learning company. In fact, it might be impeded by too great a reliance on training; it might be led into meeting today's problem with yesterday's solution, unless the object of the training is to create flexibility.

They go on to emphasise that a learning organisation provides a climate where all the individual members are encouraged to learn and develop their full potential. They move well beyond mere competence. The learning culture is also extended to all stakeholders, e.g. suppliers and customers, so that inter-dependencies are created. Human resource development is seen as central to the company strategy.

The CEO of IBM is quoted as saying, 'Our business is learning and we sell the byproducts of that learning'. This is a powerful statement, which just about sums up all that can be said about the learning organisation. It actually says that when you are working, whatever your job, the whole purpose is to learn, which means changing understanding and approaches. Arising from this, something – either goods or services – is produced for the customers. The activity which produced it was *learning*.

Pedler, Boydell and Burgoyne see the continuous process of organisational transformation as harnessing the outcomes of individual learning to change the culture and methods of the company, so that it is more responsive to whatever may be required to succeed. The changes develop from within rather than being the result of external intervention. This is all about intelligent people intelligently employed, with working practices which support the approach.

Bob Garratt (1987) speaks of learning as the key developable and tradable commodity of an organisation; and what we have been describing, particularly in Chapter 8, shows that it is not merely a matter of being nice to people or being altruistic. It is the key to competitive edge and business success.

What is a learning organisation?

In the same mood as the Pedler, Boydell and Burgoyne material is the following set of statements, taken from a workshop held to discuss management development under the auspices of the Ashridge Management Research Group. These just emerged from group discussions among forty-five people who had a wide variety of backgrounds.

A learning organisation is an organisation which:

- aims to enable its people to adapt and change
- constantly renews itself
- has people who are ready to learn new skills and methods
- understands and encourages learning processes
- develops support systems, resource centres, etc.
- encourages curiosity
- sees the line manager role as to develop staff, including 'shop floor', encouraging them to learn, encouraging them to come up with ideas
- recognises every assignment as a learning opportunity
- looks outward and encourages this
- rewards, recognises, and develops managers who do develop others
- doesn't assume the boss has all answers
- helps 'everyone' to identify and use learning opportunities

- does not segregate functions – sees the whole business as everyone's business, not just their own function; helps them to understand the big picture
- talks a lot and listens even more
- uses coaching opportunities all the time
- communicates effectively – both ways
- is open – honest – engenders trust
- learns from both success and failure
- tolerates failure, provided learning is gained from it
- reduces barriers to learning
- everyone seems to understand customer needs
- links with suppliers and customers in mutual learning
- learns what is going on all the time: all in it are on a journey, all transferring information to each other and to stakeholders, all the time
- has hunger to learn
- sees learning as implicit in all 'doing' at all levels from shop floor to board

What to do to make an organisation into a learning one (learningful companies)

1 Recognise where organisation is now.
2 Establish common purpose – *vision* – *mission*.
3 Ensure everyone knows where they fit into (2): their part – roles and responsibilities – objectives.
4 Establish value set, which includes commitment to learning.
5 Do something to reinforce all this.
6 Review whether this has convinced everyone.
7 Use business-related projects in groups.
8 Help line managers develop coaching skills and include abilities to advise on selection of learning material.
9 Help everyone to learn how to learn more efficiently.
10 Actively use job rotation.
11 Provide forums to exchange views.
12 Implement reward systems to encourage individual contributions and learning (and managers for developing others).
13 Make cross-functional collaboration a way of life.

[170]

14 Involve everyone in reviews of mission, goals, environment.
15 See TQM, quality circles, continuous improvement, suggestion schemes as learning opportunities.
16 Use appraisal mainly for development purposes.
17 Remember business unit autonomy.

The excellence theme and the learning organisation

'The learning organisation' is not a Tom Peters phrase, yet he is really always talking about it, and when we want to illustrate the learning organisation in our programme 'Making Change Work' at Ashridge, we often use his video film *The Leadership Challenge.*

His book *Thriving on Chaos* is notable for its forty-five prescriptions for a world turned upside-down. Tom Peters is, in effect, always writing about change, and whether you are a disciple or just irritated by his evangelical style, you have to admit that he has influenced the approach to business in a radical way.

He portrays organisations which are totally dedicated to the customer, concerned to provide quality of service and product, and caring about people, whether customer, supplier or employee. At the end of each chapter he suggests a series of first steps that might be taken to start down the path he is proposing. He is describing an organisation in which everything done in the job is aiming not only to meet the current demand but to improve the product or service.

Peters and other authors we have quoted recognise that, as people work, they learn how to do better what they are doing, how to work together as a team; in many cases they actually are given responsibility for figuring out how to do the job. They learn on the job how to do what needs doing, how to co-operate and how to do it better. They will be full of curiosity about why things are as they are and why couldn't they be better? They will constantly come up with new ideas and will always be searching out information that will help them along the improvement path.

This atmosphere will permeate the whole organisation. It will be present on the shop floor, behind the store counter,

[171]

among the sales force, as well as in foremen, and junior and middle managers. It can be present at these levels without there being a company policy which requires this approach. People have more power to change things than they sometimes think they have. Nevertheless, if the same attitude permeates the boardroom and senior management, then there is a much better chance of the organisation being a true learning organisation. With drive from the top, the organisation will take on a life of its own in relation to learning and all that this implies. Synergy will be manifest and the total learning will be greater than the sum of the individual components, though the individuals still matter as individuals and as groups within the wider context.

Specifics for action

The specifics in these processes consist largely of getting managers at various levels to take a definite step in the next few days or weeks. So you might go out and discover information about the customer or the environment; hold intensive meetings with all the stakeholders to learn what customers want, what suppliers can do, what the workers' perspectives are; and so on. This means learning: learning about the real definition, in the customers' terms, of quality, of uniqueness of product or service; learning about the international market; about what motivates people; about intangible benefits.

It means listening: listening to all stakeholders, to anyone who can give you a useful insight into any aspect of the business. This means being out there in the world, not stuck behind the desk all the time. It calls for the encouragement of learning by reinforcement with reward, praise and support. It means ceaseless discussion of the outcomes of all this activity, with learning made intentional rather than accidental. It includes risk-taking and experimentation, and keeping the ear to the ground for good ideas that other people, including competitors, are having.

Learning organisations don't hug information to themselves, and even lend their people to other parts of the organisation to aid projects as well as widen experiences. They are also networks of co-operation and idea-sharing, and they buy into other external networks to enhance the learning process. They are places where the killer phrases which prevent progress and inhibit learning are rarely heard. Everyone is made aware of their value and put into the mood to contribute and be a member of what some companies have called the 'crew'. They look for short cuts and reduction of paperwork. They assume that what has existed for a long while is probably outmoded and due for a change.

Learning organisations are inspired by a vision, a sense of purpose and meaning. They have role models and mentors from whom they may learn. They are not status conscious. All can learn from each. All are colleagues and fellow-learners, who can learn not least from those at the sharp end of the enterprise. These organisations love change and are places where change and learning are almost synonymous. They have a sense of urgency and are places where laughter is frequently heard. It makes a good atmosphere for learning.

The leadership challenge

Maybe this sounds a little over the top and idealistic, but the Peters video film of four enterprises gives credibility to the ideals. We here see the principles in operation, of people on the shop floor being given the opportunity to run their own show and to gain a sense of ownership, along the lines we have illustrated in Chapter 8.

Workers no longer have to park their brains at the door; leaders share power and information with the workers and thereby give them the tools to do the job, the ability to learn as they work what needs to be done. Managers cease to hoard information and power. They enable others to know how their small parts fit into the wider picture, so that they feel more significant. In a General Motors plant, 'suddenly the pent-up energy of 2000 energetic, creative, intelligent, thoughtful, adult human beings was put in the service of making better products and holding on to a job . . .'

The film on Johnsonville Foods shows the work of self-managed teams, who do their own hiring and training and develop and control their own quality and productivity to standards far higher than any centralised bureaucracy could instil, because they have figured them out for themselves, because they are learning all the time how to improve. This is very much the approach of the quality circle movement at its best, and the Japanese passion for *kaizen*, a term which means continuous improvement and a bit more. At Johnsonville managers are called co-ordinators. One of them says: 'We're teachers, we help people grow. My main goal is to help people grow so they can handle all the situations in the plant on their own' (just like Rothmans).

These companies also encourage all forms of individual learning as a lifelong activity, on the grounds that employees who are growing in any way will be more effective at the job. The chief executive of one of them says he doesn't really run the place: 'I'm in charge of philosophy. I'm in charge of setting the standards, making sure we're on the right track. I'm in charge of defining the values'. When he says he is in charge, that doesn't mean he does those things without a lot of input from everyone else. He stimulates what the whole organisation does.

Self-esteem is high in these organisations. Rules and regulations are minimal, yet discipline is high.

The international learning organisation

The learning organisation theme also has an international context. It is important to include this aspect with the growing internationalisation of business. A further source of information about learning organisations is *Managing Across Borders* by Bartlett and Ghoshal (1989). We summarise its key points.

Traditionally there have been three broad categories of international companies:

1 The *multi-national*, which tends to be an accumulation of largely independent subsidiaries which are left in many respects to get on with the job of responding to local needs as worked out by the people on the spot. Such subsidiaries are sensitive to the national differences between the country in which they operated and the home country. They formed strong local presences. Unilever and Philips are given as examples.

[174]

2 The *global*, which is strongly controlled from the corporate centre and builds cost advantage through centralised global operations. The world is treated as a global whole which needs essentially the same products, or can be made to see such a need. Global efficiency is the keynote, not local diversity. Often products are developed at home and then produced and/or sold on a standard basis overseas. Matsushita is given as an example. Its expansion overseas was through an export-based strategy, and it retains strong centralised product development, manufacturing operations and marketing strategy.

3 The strategy of the third type of company, termed *international* by the authors, is based primarily on transferring and adapting the parent company's knowledge or expertise to foreign markets. The parent retains considerable influence and control, but national companies can adapt products and ideas coming from the centre. These companies are based on the worldwide exploitation of knowledge, and for distinction the authors call them international companies. Ericsson's are picked out as a successful example of this kind of company, which achieves its success by the effectiveness of its transfer of its knowledge and competencies. This third category describes a learning organisation in the most strategic sense, which does not mean that in detail it displays the characteristics of which we have been speaking.

By the mid-1980s no company working across national borders could afford to stick to just one of the above three categories. Global integration, local differentiation and worldwide innovation had all become compelling requirements. 'To compete effectively, a company had to develop global competitiveness, multinational flexibility and worldwide learning capability simultaneously.'

This meant multiple strategic competencies were required, and traditional management modes had to be broken away from. 'The challenge of building a learning and self-adaptive organisation which was also competitive and flexible, involved a range of tasks.' This fourth category is the most comprehensive of the learning organisations, and Bartlett and Ghoshal term it the *transnational*.

They say that essentially the transnational company is a new management mentality. The detailed section of the book describes how the characteristics of global scale, local responsiveness, and worldwide diffusion and adaptation can be interwoven by the concept of the learning organisation. This is learning at the highest and most comprehensive level, but it fits in well with what our other authors have said about the learning organisation embracing all levels of the company; it moves out on to a wider canvas of feedback and shared information, and learning is shuttling back and forth across the continents, so that what is learned in India may find application in, say, Nigeria. Centres of excellence are established in different countries as role models for the rest, depending on local strengths, instead of information being centralised at corporate head office.

Introducing this international element toward the end of our book may sound like starting a new one, but in principle it is identical with the picture we have been painting of the learning organisation, where *in the doing* people learn and through feedback go on to do better. Whether it is an automobile factory working cross-functionally to share with everybody the learning of everybody else, or whether it is one national subsidiary sharing its accrued knowledge with all the other subsidiaries, it is still an expression of a frame of mind and the consequence of being part of enterprises which consist of teams.

Conclusion

We have reached the stage in the book where it is customary to write a short concluding chapter, which attempts to bring the threads together. We have decided not to do this, because the theme of this chapter is the one that brings all else together.

We started with change as the norm of life, the norm of the affairs of the world in general and of business in particular. We made clear that our aim was to help readers to welcome change, to thrive on change, to initiate it and to make it serve their own prosperity and that of the whole of society.

We can only hope that we have served that purpose by seeing change within ourselves as a fundamental need, by a sense of global awareness, by heeding the call of an exciting future, by the stimulus of success stories of those who have dared to embrace change, and even by talking of 'love in the workplace'. We hope we have included you all in our suggestion that you have more power than you think you have, and that no reader will fail to tackle this very day some little thing which, along with a lot of other little things, will make a big difference.

We don't want to add much more, because we want to leave as our final message the theme of the learning organisation. We all go to work to *do* things, but the way we do them is by learning and therefore changing every minute of the day. We want to see the exciting challenge of this idea become the message of messages for the 1990s. And with it the move on from an inadequate individualism to a spirit where we all belong to teams and achieve our self-actualisation by the actualisation of the team, while still retaining the courage to stand alone if need be. Reaching forward into the future, we will even dare to hope that our children and grandchildren will combine individual courage with collective care to become members of the global team.

FOR READING AND REFERENCE

Adams, J.D., Hayes, J. and Hopson, B. (1976) *Transition, Understanding and Managing Personal Change*, London, Martin Robertson.

Albrecht, K. and Zemke, R. (1985) *Service America*, Homewood, Illinois, Dow Jones-Irwin.

Bartlett, C. and Ghoshal, S. (1989) *Managing Across Borders*, London, Hutchinson Business Books.

Bennis, W. and Nanus, B. (1985) *Leaders. The Strategies for Taking Charge*, New York, Harper & Row.

Block, P. (1988) *The Empowered Manager*, San Francisco, Jossey Bass.

Cantor, D. and Mervis, P. (1989) *The Cynical Americans*, San Francisco, Jossey Bass.

Carlzon, J. (1987) *Moments of Truth*, Cambridge, Cambridge University Press.

Cox, D. (1988) *By GABB and by GIBB*, Greenfield Assessment Burton Brewery and Greenfield Implementation Burton Brewery, Lichfield.

Critchley, B. and Casey, D. (1989) 'Organisations Get Stuck Too', *Leadership and Organisation Development Journal*, Volume 10, No. 4.

Crosby, P.B. (1978) *Quality is Free*, Maidenhead, McGraw-Hill.

Curson, C. (1986) *Flexible Patterns of Work*, Wimbledon, Institute of Personnel Management.

Davis, S. (1988) *2001 Management*, London, Simon & Schuster.

Deming, W.E. (1986) *Out of the Crisis*, Cambridge, Cambridge University Press.

Elkington, J. (1987) *The Green Capitalists*, London, Victor Gollancz.

Fiegenbaum, E. and McCorduck, P. *The Fifth Generation*, New York, Penguin.

Fiegenbaum, E. *et al.* (1988) *The Rise of the Expert Company*, London, Macmillan.

Garratt, B. (1987) *The Learning Organization*, London, Fontana.

Gleick, J. (1987) *Chaos*, London, Sphere Books.

Greiner, L. (1985) 'Classic Advice on Aspects of Organisational Life', *Harvard Business Review on Management* Volume 1, New York, Harper & Row.

Handy, C. (1989) *Age of Unreason*, London, Century Hutchinson.

Handy, C. (1984) *The Future of Work*, Oxford, Blackwell.

Harris, P.R. (1985) *Management in Transaction*, San Francisco, Jossey Bass.

Harrison, R. (1987) *Organisation Culture and Quality of Service: A strategy for releasing love in the workplace*, London, Association for Management Education and Development.

Harvey-Jones, J. (1988) *Making it Happen*, London, Collins.

Hornstein, H. (1986) *Managerial Courage*, Chichester, John Wiley.

Juran, J.M. (1964) *Managerial Breakthrough*, Maidenhead, McGraw-Hill.

Keen, P.G.W. (1988) *Competing in Time*, Cambridge, Mass., Ballinger.

Kirkpatrick, D. (1985) *How to Manage Change Effectively*, San Francisco, Jossey Bass.

Kolb, D. (1984) *Experiental Learning*, Englewood Cliffs, NJ, Prentice-Hall.

Kotter, J.P. (1985) *Power and Influence beyond Formal Authority*, New York, Macmillan.

Kouzes, J.M. and Posner, B.Z. (1987) *The Leadership Challenge*, San Francisco, Jossey Bass.

Levinson, D. (1978) *The Seasons of a Man's Life*, New York, Random House.

Mead, G.H. (1962) *Mind, Self and Society*, University of Chicago Press.

Morgan, G. (1988) *Riding the Waves of Change*, San Francisco, Jossey Bass.

Naisbitt, J. and Aburdene, P. (1990) *Megatrends 2000*, London, Sidgwick & Jackson.

Pedler, M., Boydell, T. and Burgoyne, J. (1989) *Toward the Learning Company*, Volume 20, Part 1, MEAD, London Association of Management Education and Development.

Peters, T. (1987) *Thriving on Chaos*, New York, A.A. Knopf.

Peters, T.J. and Waterman, R.H. (1982) *In Search of Excellence: Lessons from America's Best-Run Companies*, New York, Harper & Row.

Pilditch, J. (1987) *Winning Ways*, London, Mercury Books.

Revans, R.W. (1982) *Original and Growth of Action Learning*, Bromley, Kent, Chartwell-Bratt.

Rogers, B. (1987) *Getting the Best Out of Yourself and Others*, New York, Harper & Row.

Sales, L. and Strauss, G. (1966) *Human Behaviour in Organisations*, Englewood Cliffs, N.J., Prentice Hall.

Schein, E. (1978) *Career Dynamics*, Reading, Mass., Addison-Wesley.

Spencer, S.A. and Adams, J.D. (1990) *Life Changes: Growing through personal transitions*, San Luis, Obispo, Ca., Impact Publishers.

Stewart, R. (1982) *Choices*, London, McGraw-Hill.

Stewart, V. (1983) *Change, the Challenge for Management*, London, McGraw-Hill.

Watzlawick, P. *et al* (1974) *Change, Principles of Problem Formation and Resolution*, New York, W.W. Norton.

Weisbord, M.R. (1987) *Productive Workplaces*, San Francisco, Jossey Bass.

Whitehead, A.N. (1978) *Process and Reality*, corrected edition, London, Collier Macmillan.

Wickens, P. (1987) *The Road to Nissan*, Basingstoke, Macmillan.

Wille, E. (1990) *People Development and Improved Business Performance*, Berkhamsted. Ashridge Management Research Group.

Wille, E. (1989) *Triggers for Change*, Berkhamsted, Ashridge Management Research Group.

Woodward, H. and Buckholz, S. (1987) *Aftershock, Helping People through Corporate Change*, Chichester, John Wiley.

INDEX

[181]